# JIM WIDEMAN

# STRETCH

## Structuring Your Ministry for Growth

**An Infuse Publication**

©2011 Jim Wideman Ministries, Inc

2441 Q Old Fort Parkway #354

Murfreesboro, TN 37128

**www.jimwideman.com**

This book is dedicated to all the wonderful
kidmin leaders of Infuse.

Thanks for making me a better leader
and letting me watch your dreams come
true, which in turn is making some of my
dreams come true.
I love you all!

# TABLE OF CONTENTS

# ACKNOWLEDGMENTS

In 2008, I started my very first coaching and mentoring group (a.k.a. Infuse) as a way to fulfill God's call on my life to pass on my experience to the next generation of children's ministry leaders. It has been rewarding, as well as, amazing to watch how God has assembled all eight groups I've had the privilege to do life with. I want to give special thanks to Jenny Funderburke, Spencer Click, Jen Galley, Sam Luce and Sara Richards who presently assist me as coaches.

I also want to thank my wonderful family for letting me open our home to kidmin folks from all over the U.S. Thanks for your endless love and support and for being my greatest sermon.

Also this book would not exist without Jenny Funderburke's help, encouragement, and hard work. Thanks for convincing me to teach this information in a day-trip conference so we could make this book possible, and thank you also for all the hours you invested in transcribing the lessons and helping me get this information from my heart to the printed page. Thanks for your love and support and for being a big part of Team Jim.

Also, a big thanks goes to Pastor Allen Jackson and the wonderful Next Generation staff and teams of World Outreach Church. It is such an honor to be a part of what God is doing in Middle Tennessee.

## chpt 1:
# THE IMPORTANCE OF STRUCTURE

If you are reading this book and you are in ministry, chances are you're praying one of these three prayers:

1. *"Dear Lord, please don't send any more children. We are just hanging on by the skin of our teeth."*

Is that you? You love kids and want them to come to know the Lord, but you just can't handle any more? You are barely hanging on from Sunday to Sunday? Well, this book is for you.

2. *"Lord, I really want You to send me some more kids. Why aren't You sending me more kids?"*

You feel like you have a great ministry. Your passion is to see more kids come to know the Lord. But something must be missing because the kids aren't coming, or when they do, they aren't sticking. This book is for you too.

3. *"Lord, You're sending the kids . . . now HELP!"*

You might be in the middle of phenomenal growth and feel you are just barely keeping your head above water. You need more space, you need more time, you need more volunteers, and in fact, another *you* would be nice. Well, then this book is for you.

Wherever you are in ministry, improving your structure is the key to being ready for the next stage God has for you. The right structure can keep you from being afraid of growth. The wrong structure can keep growth from happening. Improving your structure can allow growth to continue. What you do now really is going to matter later.

# THE IMPORTANCE OF STRUCTURE

When you dream about the future of your ministry, what do you see? Do you imagine a skyscraper, solid and secure reaching new heights, or a shack, shaky and unstable just hoping to make it another day? That's probably a dumb question to ask. No one hopes to have a ministry that can fall apart at any moment. We all strive to do the very best we can to accomplish God's purposes for the children He has put in our care. So, what are you doing now to prepare for that ministry God has called you to?

The key to any building is its **foundation**. Just because you want to build a five-story building, doesn't mean you can. If you don't have the right foundation, there's no way you'll be able to build what you want to build. You usually don't notice the foundation of a building when you look at it. You see the outside—the color, the architecture, the bricks, or the wood. Ministry is the same way. A lot of times people will just look at the outward things without really understanding there is a whole lot that happens in the foundation that either causes you to see your dreams come true or causes you to come up short.

Do you remember the story from the Bible of the wise man and the foolish man? You know, the one you've heard your whole life and have taught to kids in children's church. Let's look at that familiar story in Matthew 7:24-29. The story goes that the first guy didn't build his house on a rock; he built it on the sand, and when the winds and the waters and the floods came, his house wasn't able to handle it. He didn't build on a good foundation.

Matthew 7:25 tells us about the wise man's house. "The rain came down, the streams rose, and the winds blew and beat against that house; yet it did not fall, because it had its foundation on the rock." This guy did it right. He took the time to build on a foundation that was solid and secure. As time passed and as challenging times came, his house stood tall.

What does this story have to do with children's ministry (other than the song that you are probably singing in your head right now)? The right foundation makes a difference in what we build for God. The type of foundation determines what you're able to build. In many ways, the future of your ministry depends on the foundation you are building right now.

In children's ministry, that foundation is the structure you create. Often, ministers think they can create children's ministry success by the décor of their building or their cool check-in system or their cutting-edge programming. All of that is good, but it won't last. If that is what you are building your ministry on, you are building it on sand. When the right storm blows up, your ministry is at risk of crashing down. Or even worse, it might not ever get built in the first place.

When Jesus started His earthly ministry, the very first thing He did was establish structure. He immediately chose twelve men whom we call the disciples. The first thing Jesus did was use the twelve to establish structure and build something of value. He proves you can't do the workload by yourself. And if the Son of God needed help, you and I need tons of it.

# TWO FORMS OF STRUCTURE

I mainly classify structure in two forms. The first is a **growth structure**; this is the one you want to have so you are able to grow. But what stops growth is the other kind of structure—maintenance structure. A **maintenance structure** will swallow up your growth structure.

Allow me to explain. Here in America, when you are 75-80 percent full, you are full. This is not always true in other countries, but it is true here. A seven-passenger minivan will only hold five Americans, but in Uganda, a seven-passenger minivan can hold up to thirty people. I saw it with my own eyes when I was there a few years ago. In America, once your growth structure hits 75-80 percent, you have entered maintenance mode, and the only fix is to enlarge your growth structure.

I discovered this at my very first church. When I started in children's ministry, seven kids attended my children's church (six normal kids and a little boy named Bubba). I believed God wanted us to grow, so I put together a plan and a strategy to reach a hundred kids. The closer I got to a hundred, the harder it was to break through. In fact, I got stuck at seventy-five. What I did not realize then was my growth structure had just turned into a maintenance structure with no help from me. I was stuck, and if I wanted to blow past a hundred children, I had to be willing to change my structure.

Although I had not hit a hundred yet in my children's ministry, I enlarged my structure to handle over two hundred children. Soon we passed right over the hundred barrier and kept growing. If you are not experiencing growth presently, it is likely because your structure is holding you back. You are stuck and swamped in a maintenance structure. You need to stretch.

Most of us really do want growth, even if we are scared of it. We want God to send us more kids and more families. We want to share the Gospel, we want more salvations, and we want more of a movement of God. But let me ask you a question: if He sent those things to you this Sunday, would you be ready? If a hundred new families walked into your church, would you know what to do with them? Would their kids have teachers? Would they even have a classroom? If fifty people who wanted to serve approached you this Sunday, could your system handle it?

**That's what structure is all about.**

Growth structure means you are organized in such a way that you can better handle what God sends your way. Maintenance structure means you are organized in a way that gets you by from Sunday to Sunday. Growth structure means you are thinking ahead and creating systems that will last as God sends you the growth. Maintenance structure means you are thinking, *This is what we've always done.* When you structure for growth, you are creating a foundation of rock that keeps your ministry stable through whatever storms God sends along.

Let me ask you another question. Why would God send you growth if you aren't prepared for it? Why would He send you a boatload of new families if you don't have a system to care for and follow up on them? Why would God entrust you with a lot of salvations if you aren't ready to follow up on decisions? Why would God send you dozens of new volunteers if you aren't structured in a way that creates a good service environment for them?

Some of your ministries are already growing, and you are about to pull your hair out. You are stressed out. People are frustrated. You are running like crazy. And eventually, all of that stress will stop the growth.

It's kind of like what you do about your pants when you start gaining weight. You either get bigger pants, or you lose weight. The same is true in ministry: if we don't get bigger pants (a bigger structure), then all of the structure starts choking out the growth that is happening.

# THREE KEYS TO GROWTH

## 1. EXPAND YOUR STRUCTURE

The first thing that we have to do before our ministries can grow is expand our structure. Isaiah 54:2-3 says, "Enlarge the place of your tent, stretch your tent curtains wide, do not hold back; lengthen your cords, strengthen your stakes. For you will spread out to the right and to the left."

I will be talking about this a lot in the coming chapters, but first you must understand that **for growth to happen, you have to make room for it**. You have to intentionally expand various parts of your ministry so that you will be ready.

## 2. KEEP DOING WHAT BROUGHT YOU SUCCESS

When you're setting yourself up for growth, you don't do everything new. You keep doing the things that brought you success. Galatians 6:9 says, "Let us not become weary in doing good, for at the proper time we will reap a harvest if we do not give up." I like to say it this way: you've got to dance with the girl who brought you. What has your ministry been doing that you believe God has blessed? Outreach? Friendliness? Serving the community? Focusing on families? Tech-savvy environments? There is a reason God has been blessing you and wants to send you growth. Pray and seek to identify the good that you are doing, and keep doing it!

## 3. DON'T DO THE SAME STUFF

On the flip side, the third key to growth is to not do the same stuff. Same actions bring same results. If you want something you've never had, you've got to be willing to act differently. If I want to lose weight, I can't eat the same things I ate to gain the weight. It's the same with growth: you can't keep doing the same things and think you're going to get different results. Isaiah 43:19 says, "See, I am doing a new thing! Now it springs up; do you not perceive it?"

# BECOME A STUDENT OF STRUCTURE

So, are you ready to get started? Your first step is one that will never end. You must become a student of structure. Second Timothy 2:15 KJV says, "Study to show thyself approved." This verse applies to the Word, but it also applies to structure.

## STUDY OTHER CHURCHES

Do your homework. If you're a church of 300 and you want to grow to a church of 500 or 800, find some churches that have children's ministries around that size, and see if you can get a hold of their flowcharts. Every church has different structures and strategies they bring to the table.

When I moved to Murfreesboro, the care for workers was just second to none. They had a position that I in thirty years of ministry to four other churches had never heard of—a team leader. All that team leader did was help pastor the other volunteers by making sure they're doing okay, praying for them if they're sick, or organizing food if they have baby. The way our volunteers take care of each other here is the most amazing thing. That team leader helps care for and pastor that group. I certainly learned something new at this church, and you can learn from other churches too.

## CONNECT WITH OTHERS

Are you an island, or are you part of a community? In this day and age, there are tons of ways to connect with children's ministers all over the world. For example, I love conferences because I love connecting with other people and asking questions about what they are doing. Find you some children's ministers, and ask them lots of questions about how they structure their ministries. Take every opportunity to learn what people are doing in other churches.

## SHARE FLOWCHARTS

Once you've connected with others, share flowcharts with them. Send your flowcharts to other children's ministers, and collect theirs.

I shouldn't have to tell this to people who work at a church, but I do. Check with the people you actually work with. Check with other departments, and ask about their flowcharts. Sometimes we look outside of the church instead of inside our own church. If there is a department that is really clicking, find out what they do. If preschool has been doing really well but the elementary isn't, the elementary person should ask the preschool person what they're doing.

## STUDY CORPORATIONS

It doesn't have to just be churches, you can learn from businesses too. Most business practices are from the book of Proverbs; it's just that most people don't know which chapter and verse they are from. Some of my favorite people are people who bring me policy-and-procedure books from corporations. I enjoy a good policies-and-procedures book. I like to hang out with HR people. In fact, my idea of a good time is somebody's insurance policies.

Study every practical business book you can get your hands on. One of my favorite books is *Sam Walton: Made in America.* In that book, Sam gives away some of his success secrets. He says that one of the corporations he structured Wal-Mart™ after was IBM™ because of how they pushed authority down and watched out for bureaucracy. If the largest retailer in America studied other businesses, we should too.

## STUDY STRUCTURE IN THE BIBLE

When you become a student of structure, you'll see the number twelve is associated with government, (e.g., the twelve tribes of Israel and the twelve apostles). That's the reason I've tried not to have more than twelve direct reports at one time. Examine how Jesus leads and structures His team. Study the wisdom that fills the book of Proverbs.

## ALWAYS SEEK GOD

The last thing I'll mention before we dive into the details of creating structure is the most important. If you do this alone, it doesn't matter how great of a structure you create: it will be built on sand. Don't ever forget that Psalm 127:1 tells us, "Unless the Lord builds the house, its builders labor in vain." We aren't looking to build what we think is best. We want to follow God's direction and vision for our ministries. We want Him to be the builder. Never forget we are just in sales. Our God is in management.

*chpt 2:*
# MAKING ROOM TO RECEIVE

There are two words that I don't pay attention to anymore—*big* and *busy*. Their definitions change all the time. What I used to think of as *big* is not *big* to me today. And what I think is *big* today isn't what I am going to think is *big* down the road, so I don't use the word. *Busy* is another word I've learned not to say. Have you ever thought you couldn't get any busier, and then you woke up? Both are very relative terms.

But I've learned something that's key in structuring for growth. God has promised He will never put more on you than you can handle (1 Cor. 10:13). Whenever I have a lot that I have to do on my plate, I thank the Lord that He thinks more of me than I. I ask Him to help me agree with Him. Obviously, if He put it on my plate and I heard a *thus saith the Lord* for me to do it, then I have to say "Alright Lord, obviously *You* think I can handle this; and if you think I can handle this, I choose to agree with you." I have to make room to receive what He is calling me to do.

There are different types of words from God that I need at different points in my walk with Him. There are times I need inspiration, and there are times I need vision. There are times I need to learn a method, but then there are times I need to learn a principle. This chapter is about the key principle for structuring for growth: you have to make room for it.

God will give you what you make room for. He is the Good Steward. He never puts things on us and then says, "Let's watch them crash and burn." That's not how the Lord works. So, if there's something we need to do, then I believe that the same God that gave us the assignment will facilitate and help us through it.

When you have a direct assignment from Jesus, He will equip you. He always equips those He calls. So when you are working on a project, you have to ask yourself, "Is it God or gas? Is it last night's pepperoni pizza or is it *thus saith the Lord*?" Have you heard from God? If you know it is from God, then He is going to help you. But there are things you need to do too.

When we study Scripture, we see a formula for how God wants us to work alongside of Him to make room for what He wants us to do. Let's look at two of Jesus' familiar miracles, starting with the very first miracle He did as recorded in **John 2:1-5**:

> *On the third day a wedding took place at Cana in Galilee. Jesus' mother was there and Jesus and his disciples had also been invited to the wedding. When the wine was gone, Jesus' mother said to him, "They have no more wine."*
>
> *"Woman, why do you involve me?" Jesus replied. "My time has not yet come."*

*His mother said to the servants, "Do whatever he tells you."*

(Here's a free side note: Jesus is in His thirties yet his mother is still involved, which means you never get done parenting. It is different, but it is still parenting. This story shows us the best kind of parenting. Jesus says He isn't going to do anything, but Mary knows her son will do the right thing, so she walks off. She doesn't nag or fuss. Sometimes, parents have to believe their kids will do the right thing, and then they have to give them the opportunity to make the right choice.)

Now, let's get back to the story. Verse six says, *"Nearby stood six stone water jars, the kind used by the Jews for ceremonial washing, each holding from twenty to thirty gallons."*

Being a detail guy, I had to know what this really meant. Water weighs about 8.33 pounds per gallon. That means each stone jar held 167-250 pounds of water. Do you realize that some physical work was involved in carrying those bad boys? I also know from going to Israel that most of the banquet rooms were upstairs. There were stairs involved! Not only that, the water systems in these ancient cities provided water from a central source, so unless that banquet room happened to be right next to that source, there was a journey involved too.

Jesus set up this miracle so that people had to do some physical work that didn't involve anything spiritual or mystical. The practical application is most of the time, ministry looks a whole lot like work. There are people who are more talented than me and who are a lot better looking, but no one has to outwork me.

Let's continue. John 2:7 says, *"Jesus said to the servants, 'Fill the jars with water'; so they filled them to the brim."* You know, if it had been me, I would have said, "Are you sure we need all this water? If we do fill to the brim, can't we just do half the jars?" I would have negotiated, but they obeyed Jesus. He said fill them up, so they filled them up; and they received a blessing to the brim.

> *Then he told them, "Now draw some out and take it to the master of the banquet."*
>
> *They did so, and the master of the banquet tasted the water that had been turned into wine. He did not real-ize where it had come from, though the servants who had drawn the water knew.*

Jesus asked the same people who put the water in the jars to draw some out and serve it as wine. No one except the master of the banquet expected there to be wine in there. This was a step of faith. Can't you hear them asking, "So, you want me to draw water and pass it off to that old boy as wine?" Can you imagine how hard that first step was?

I don't know exactly when the miracle took place, but I know how the Lord has worked in my life. He has never been late, but He has seldom been early. In the Jim version, when that guy let go of the cup and the master took the cup, that is when it turned into wine.

Let's examine one more miracle and see similar steps, and then we will discuss the equation we see in Scripture for making room to receive the big things God has for us. Look at the miracle of the feeding of the five thousand. We know this story was especially im-portant because it is the only one that is told in all four gospels.

*When Jesus landed and saw a large crowd, he had
compassion on them and healed their sick. As evening
approached, the disciples came to him and said, "This
is a remote place, and it's already getting late. Send
the crowds away, so they can go to the villages and buy
themselves some food."*

*Jesus replied, "They do not need to go away. You give
them something to eat."*
**Matthew 14:14-16**

There's that direct assignment from Jesus: *thus saith the Lord*. It
continues, *"'We have here only five loaves of bread and two fish,'
they answered"* (v. 17). Isn't it interesting that before the guys tell
Jesus to turn the people away, they have already taken inventory?
I think they were not only worried about what they were going to
eat, but I think Jesus had already taught them to come prepared
when there's a major decision to be made.

*"Bring them here to me," he said. And he directed the
people to sit down on the grass. Taking the five loaves
and the two fish and looking up to heaven, he gave
thanks and broke the loaves. Then he gave them to the
disciples, and the disciples gave them to the people.*
**Matthew 14:18-19**

Before Jesus prays or does anything spiritual, He makes a plan.
Mark's gospel tells us He had the people sit down in hundreds and
fifties. It doesn't matter if you're using a catering truck or a little

boy's lunch, you need a plan for how people are going to get fed. And you need to be able to give direction.

When you are outside without a PA system, someone can get overlooked. But you can easily walk up and see if fifty people have not been fed yet. Jesus has a physical plan carried out before He calls on God. God didn't have to speak and tell them to get in groups of fifty: the disciples took care of that. They are calling on God to do the miracle. God doesn't ever expect you to do what you can't, but He does expect you to do what you physically can do.

The story continues, *"They all ate and were satisfied, and the disciples picked up twelve basketfuls of broken pieces that were left over"* (v. 20). Here the disciples take a step of faith by giving the food to the people. They know how much they have, yet they step out and start handing out bread and fish. That is a risk. And you know what? A lot of people aren't willing to take risks to grow.

People always worry and say, "What if I fail?" Here's a better question, **what if you accomplish it?** There is a risk in starting a new campus, starting a new service, or allowing people to teach who haven't taught before. All of that is a risk, but it is a good risk when God is in it!

Not only do we have a principle from these stories of Jesus' miracles, but now we have a formula:

## STEP I: IDENTIFY THE PROBLEM.

What is the problem? This answer will help you come up with the right structure. At the wedding, the problem was that the party was out of wine. In the feeding of the five thousand, there were a couple of problems. Jesus and the disciples were surrounded by lots of hungry people, and there was very little food to be found.

Sometimes your problem isn't just one problem. Sometimes it is several problems, but you can't solve them all at the same time. You have to learn to prioritize.

## STEP 2: INVENTORY YOUR RESOURCES.

Do you have the stuff? Do you have the people? Do you have the rooms? Do you have enough chairs? You can't add a hundred more people if they don't have a place to sit. Sometimes the building will hold it, but a purchase may be involved. If you are preparing for adding more kids, you'll need more curriculum and more snack crackers.

## STEP 3: COME UP WITH A PLAN.

There are things God wants you to do before He intercedes and sends the miracle. Jesus had men carry big, heavy jugs of water. He had the disciples make a plan to organize all those people before there was any food. What is the part that you can do without spiritual intervention?

## STEP 4: COMMIT THAT PLAN TO GOD AND LET HIM TWEAK IT.

Don't be stupid enough to start thinking that you can do it on your own. Pray about the details of your plan. Let the Holy Spirit show you details you're missing or steps that just won't work. Don't just say, "Here's what I'm doing, now bless it." Seek His heart and His input.

## STEP 5: STEP OUT IN FAITH AND OBEDIENCE AND DO WHAT YOU CAN DO.

You've got a plan, now do it! You can't produce supernatural results, but just like in both of these stories, there are things you can step out and do now.

## STEP 6: WATCH GOD DO WHAT YOU CAN'T.

Here's the beauty of serving the one true God. He shows up and does more than we could ever ask or imagine. (Eph. 3:20.) When you've been faithful to do your part, He is faithful to do His.

## STEP 7: ENJOY THE OVERFLOW AND THE LEFTOVERS.

There was risk in both of these miracles, and it paid off because God is the God of leftovers. (I like a good meatloaf sandwich. In fact, I think I like it better than the meatloaf.) Enjoy the blessings that God sends your way. Listen to and write down the stories. Share the wins with others. Praise Him for what He does. But don't, for a minute, think that you're done—now is the time to figure out the next place to expand and do it again. Too many times, we do it one time, and then we keep putting it on our annual calendar until Jesus comes back. It is time to start back at step one and make room again.

## WHAT DO YOU WANT TO RECEIVE?

Now that you know the formula, the next question is, what do you want to receive?

# ATTENDANCE

So, you want to grow in attendance? There are several things that you need to evaluate and inventory to determine if you have room to receive more kids. First, do you have room for growth? Where are you going to put all of those kids? Do you have the workers you need to love those kids? Do you have the stuff you need? Do you have enough chairs, materials, and equipment?

Do you have a follow-up plan that facilitates growth? God changed my life when He asked me one question: "Why should I give you more if you're not taking care of what you have?"

I don't care if you're a big church or a small church, when you call someone and say, "We noticed you haven't been here and wanted to pray with you"; it blows people away. No one cares what you know until they know you care, and that's the bottom line. A big part of whether or not you can grow is if you are going to take care of the people God sends.

Why should Jesus send someone to your church if you aren't going to take care of him or her? He'll send them to someone's church that has a follow-up plan. Being a good country boy, I know that the harvest isn't complete when you pull something out of the ground. The harvest is complete when you can get it into the barn and do something with it. The same thing is true with attendance.

Along those same lines, you need to evaluate how you are bringing in prospects or visitors. What are you doing to generate new people? If you want to grow in attendance, then you need to generate leads and follow up on them. Every good salesman needs leads.

## WORKERS

This Sunday would you like to have a hundred people walk up to you and say they are ready to serve in children's ministry? Let me tell you why that won't happen. Could you automatically put one-hundred people to work without any extra work on your part? Do you already have the positions, the job descriptions, the flowcharts; and you're just waiting for them to show up? Probably not, and that's why they aren't showing up. Jesus has already promised you He won't put more on you than you can handle.

You also have to have a plan to recruit. Recruiting new volunteers doesn't happen by accident. God wants to send you people, but if you don't have a plan that you are constantly working and evaluating, He isn't likely going to send them your way. As you recruit, remember it is key to establish depth at all key positions.

## SALVATIONS

Of course we want to see more kids come to know Jesus as their Savior. That is definitely a God thing, but there are things that He lets us do to set the stage. First of all, do you offer altar calls or provide other opportunities for kids to accept salvation? It is amazing how many more people respond when you actually give them a chance. Do you have people ready and trained to talk to kids who make decisions for Christ? Do you have the follow-up materials you need?

Again, why should the Holy Spirit allow children to make life-changing decisions if you are not prepared to help them? Make sure you have Bibles, tracts, and decision cards prepared and in supply. Make sure that you have a specific plan for how you handle and follow up on salvation decisions that kids make.

## LIVE MUSIC

Do you want to add live music to your children's worship? Start with the basics. Can your PA or sound system handle the change? For every instrument or microphone you add, you have to have the channels to handle it. You have to have instruments and amps. And none of those things do you any good if you don't have the musicians to play them.

These are just a few examples of areas in your ministry where you can **make room to receive.** Identify where you can make some changes, and get busy.

## chpt 3:
# BEGINNING KEYS TO BUILDING STRUCTURE IN MINISTRY

You know you need to work on the structure of your ministry, but how in the world do you get started? There are four keys that you must keep in mind as you get started: you must have a desire to change; you must define a clear vision; you must count the cost; and you must make a plan.

## I. THE DESIRE TO CHANGE

The first key to begin building structure is having a desire to change. You can't just say, "This is the way we do it at our church." You have to be open to change! If you're not prepared to ask yourself on a regular basis: "Is there a better way to do what we're doing?" or "What are other people doing?" then you can't build a better structure.

I learned a great leadership exercise from my pastor that tests people's reactions to change. I have everyone pair off into groups of two. Then I instruct them to stand back to back and change seven things (e.g., clothes, jewelry, etc.). People fuss and fight and gripe and say all kinds of things; and I just listen. When they are done, I have them turn and face each other. The partner then has to identify the seven changes. Some folks will find all seven changes, and some folks won't.

Some people will immediately start putting everything back as it was, so I use that as an opportunity to remind them that without constant management of change, people will automatically start to put things back. It's just human nature.

Next I have them do another seven changes. For some people, it becomes easier, but others just won't do it. As I walk around and listen, I know how my leaders feel about change and if they resist it.

Lastly, I ask them to change fifty or seventy-five things. The younger the group, the more open they are to change—my college kids think it is just a big game. I use this exercise to let them know that when change is too great, people can't process it.

If you don't have a desire to change, then you need to ask God to give you that as a desire of your heart. Not wanting to be a dead church needs to be a desire of your heart as well. But the problem is some people are more comfortable with old problems than with new solutions. Is that you?

Creating growth structures is going to require some change. Some change might be major, and that would need to come from the top (i.e., from the leadership that's driving the vision in your church). Most change will require you to get out of your comfort zone and move away from doing things just like you've always done them. But it will be worth it!

# 2. DEFINE A CLEAR VISION

Second, your vision has to be defined and specific in order to create your structure. A vision is simply a picture of where you want to end up. Proverbs 29:18 says that without a vision, the people will perish. That tells me that with vision, people will flourish.

One of the reasons people start griping during the change exercise I mentioned earlier is that I just tell them to turn their backs to each other and start changing seven things. I never say why. When people don't know why they have to do things, they don't respond well. You have to paint a picture for them of where your ministry is going.

As I define my vision, I want to make sure I'm keeping with the vision of my pastor and the vision of the house. In every church, there are certain core values and beliefs that are carried throughout the church. It is important not to take your children's ministry to a place where your whole church doesn't want to go. It is your job to make sure that your vision clearly aligns with your pastor's vision.

It is also important that you define the vision for every area of your ministry. If you supervise preschool, elementary, and children's choir, then you need to have a clear vision for each area. And, as you know, there will probably be something different to work on in each area.

Your vision is very important because it dictates the kind of structure you want to build. I believe in having a large number of volunteers and finding a place for everyone to help. Therefore, my structure has to be one that enables volunteers to do that. Folks who rely on a big paid staff don't need to govern in the same way because their vision is different. Define your vision so that you can determine your structure.

As you define your vision, remember to set a pace that most of the folks can follow with you. I think most church leaders are in too much of a hurry to change. One thing people in my Infuse mentoring and coaching program always tell me, it blows them away how patient I am with change. It's because I realize that anything of value takes more time to build. The difference between a five-story building and a little lean-to is the value, and it is going to take a lot longer to build that five-story building.

## 3. COUNT THE COST

Counting the cost is the third key to beginning to build structure. Just like it's important to know where you're going, it is important to know where you're starting. Anytime you don't know where you are, you're lost. Know where you're starting.

Luke 14:28 tells us: "Suppose one of you wants to build a tower. Will he not first sit down and estimate the cost to see if he has enough money to complete it?" You have to do your homework. When counting the cost, you need to ask, "What are the needs?" Be aware as you start your homework that there are two kinds of needs. There are actual needs, and there are perceived needs. Perceived needs must be addressed just like actual needs.

You can learn an awful lot through questionnaires and interviews. Talk to everyone. Ask every leader two questions: what is working? and what is not working? I listen to workers so I can find out if the equipment, room, and facilities they are using are adequate. I want to find out what will make things better for the kids and easier for the workers to do the work of the ministry. Understanding how people perceive the ministry is important.

Being a good Southerner, I've studied war most of my life. Here's what I know about winning a war. You have to guard your supply lines. If the people who are serving you don't have what they need to excel, they cannot win. In your ministry, you have to ask where are we with supplies? Where are we with equipment? What about training? Can volunteers operate and use that equipment? That's the whole idea with the soldiers learning to dismantle a rifle. They need to totally understand what they've been given to work with. I want to increase the supplies and the skills of my people.

I like to ask the ladies at the nursery check-in window what they would change. I've even taken some little, old ladies out to lunch. I call it "Brother Jim's lunch bunch." While we're eating, I ask, "If y'all could change anything about working in the nursery, what would you change?" Then I just listen. I let them talk. They are the ones doing the work of the ministry, and I need to hear what they have to say.

When counting the cost, I interview kids. I want to find out where they are spiritually. I want to identify their needs and how we're meeting them and how we're not. Right now I have a lot of college kids who have grown up in the church I'm in. I ask them what their favorite memories are, which things helped them understand God better, and which things we need to continue for their little brothers and sisters.

I want to find out about the community I'm working in. One thing World Outreach Church has done really well is truly understanding the community of Murfreesboro, Tennessee. For you to understand where you're starting from, you need a good understanding about the culture you're working in. Not only do you need to understand it, you need to look for ways to serve and love your community. A great question we started asking years ago is if we closed our doors, would the community notice? Look for ways to bless and demonstrate the love of Jesus to your city. If you want to reach your city, you have to look for opportunities to pastor your city, not just the people who attend your church.

You also need to understand what has happened in the past. Understanding the past helps you understand people's definitions. It helps you understand their expectation levels. Sometimes what you want and what your people want are different. Plus, what your pastor wants can be a whole different thing too! In my ministry, I want to understand what each group's definition of a good ministry is. There is no way you can build something of significance until you discover what *significance* looks like.

Once you identify the needs, you have to put a priority on the needs. Watching M.A.S.H.™ over the years, I have learned about triage. Triage is the difference between what needs an operation and what needs a bandage. There are certain brochures that I have not changed since I have been here at World Outreach Church. I wanted to change them, but they were not the most pressing need. Instead, I focused on recruitment. I'd much rather have five hundred new workers than a new brochure. I couldn't say that the brochure was stunting the growth of the church, but the need for recruiting, training, depth, and structure of workers was evidently having a negative impact.

The devil attacks busy people by getting them to do stuff they have no business doing. You are the only person who can control your priorities. As Proverbs 28:2 says, "A man [woman] of understanding and knowledge maintains order." So it is important to put things in order of importance so you know what to attack and when. Once you prioritize, put it down in writing. The same Bible that tells us without vision the people perish, tells us to write the vision down and make it plain. I want to order my priorities in the form of a list.

I want to rank what's most important so I can discover what to go after first. You also should evaluate what you have to work with. Specifically, evaluate your team. What gifts and resources do you have right within your people?

The last thing to remember is counting the cost doesn't happen just once. There is no way to tell if your structure is correct if you aren't constantly evaluating. You can't fix what you have not identified as needing fixing. At my church, I constantly walk around and evaluate what is happening that is good and what needs to be fixed. The key is that I am equally committed to both.

The very first church I worked for was in Jackson, Mississippi. Jackson is one of the craziest towns because they have this stuff called Yazoo clay. Yazoo clay causes houses to shift. There were times that my family would go to bed in our little house, and during the night, the house would shift. Closets or doors that opened the day before wouldn't open. So the next morning, we'd have to go under the house to move the little jacks that supported the house to adapt to how the clay had moved.

When a foundation is moving around and things aren't stable, there's no way you can build a proper structure. It is important to evaluate on a regular basis so you know where you are.

# 4. MAKE A PLAN

Come up with a plan or blueprint. Here's what I know about Americans--if you give them a hero or a cause, people will rally around it. People follow people with a plan. Planning always needs to go before action. Any change in your structure (physical, organizational, or people-wise) needs to be something you have prayed about and made a plan for. It clearly needs to be something that is a God-idea.

First you need to make this a matter of prayer. Sometimes in ministry we plan before we pray, but we should stop and pray first. I believe God has a plan for our ministries. Matthew 6:33 reminds us, "But seek first his kingdom and his righteousness." When we've identified the needs of the ministry, we should ask the Lord to guide us to the best structure and the best way to facilitate those needs. I want to commit all of that to prayer and not lean on my own understanding.

Another way I try to not lean on my own understanding is to find out what the other people in leadership are sensing. I want to brainstorm different ideas. This is where it is so important to recognize who you have in your life.

I don't want a bunch of yes-folks who are going to tell me what I want to hear. There are times when I'm having a bad day, and those are the people I call so that they can tell me how wonderful I am. But when I want to know what it is really like, those aren't the people I'm inviting to lunch. You need to have people who you can seriously brainstorm with and who will talk straight to you. You need people who can help you formulate a plan and tell you when you are about to do something stupid.

At the same time, because you are in leadership, you see things that you don't need to share with everyone. Joseph, God love him, heard from God, but sharing that vision didn't work out so well at first. I realize that was part of God's plan, but I want you to see that sometimes people who aren't in leadership can't handle the vision. The reason that God showed your vision to you is because you're the leader. As you start looking at where you're headed, it is important that you brainstorm with people who will let you throw out ideas, but they also need to be able to handle the weight of the vision process and be a help to you.

It's important that you come up with a plan or blueprint because you need to be able to look at that long-term plan and evaluate it as you are evaluating your structure. A plan always helps you know where you are.

Do you know that architects do more than just draw plans? They walk around and inspect the work to see if it is being done according to the plan. In leading any kind of change or structure, that is why you can't spend all of your time teaching kids. You have to be out there, seeing what's going on, and making sure your team is following the plans. If what you planned wasn't good, then that's where a change order comes in. It is important that we change some of those things so that the outcome can be good.

No matter what, you need to remember to follow peace. As you make your plan, never override the checks of the Holy Spirit. If the Holy Spirit ever tells you no, and you can't explain it, you just know that you know that you know you're not supposed to do it, go with the Holy Ghost. I don't care what names they call you, how bad it gets, or what they do. The Holy Spirit is our helper, and we have to let Him help.

So many times we just ask Him to help in small things, but He wants to help in all things. If you committed this plan to prayer in the beginning, you have to be sensitive to His guidance as you get going.

The next question to ask yourself is can this plan be done in stages? There are times when you make your structure and you realize that where you need to get to is a long way from where you are. At that point, it is better to break things down into what you can do now and what you need to do later. Too much too quick is a real trick of the enemy. If it can be done in stages, establish priorities and determine first things first. One always has to go before two, and two has to go before three. It is just like putting together a bicycle for Christmas. You have to put it together in the right order, or it is going to be a mess. That's how stages fit together too. They have to be done by priorities.

Keep in mind; David didn't start with the giant. He started with the lion and the bear. In my life, I couldn't even start with the lion and the bear; I had to start with the gnat and the roach and then work my way up to other things. As you determine your plan, figure out how to tackle smaller things first, rather than doing too much at one time.

You also need to take some time to streamline ministries. Sometimes we can do too much. I think it is important to do more by doing less. First, identify the things that just aren't working. If there is something that is not bearing fruit, or you've always done it a way that doesn't exist anymore, streamline things to meet the need. Don't ride a dead horse. I don't care if you go to a seminar on how to ride a dead horse or put more money into dead-horse riding, it just isn't going to work.

I also watch out for too many babies. If you have too many things going that need all of your attention like a baby, life is going to be hard. Do you have twins or multiple births or know someone who has? There is a reason that babies typically come one at a time. When Julie and I had Yancy, we had a really good friend who had twins within days of Yancy. When we tried to get the three babies and us two couples together, I'll be honest with you, there weren't a lot of conversations going on. There were babies crawling every-where! In fact, when Yancy showed me her first sonogram of her baby, I asked if she could tell what it was. She answered, "It's not twins." That's the first thing she wanted to make sure of.

One of the things I try to tell folks in leadership is to watch out for too many babies in the crib. Let one get potty trained, and wait before you bring another into the world. Sometimes you try to have too much going at one time. Don't start a bunch of new stuff all at once. As you plan for new structure, go ahead and streamline what you're already doing. That will make a huge difference.

These four keys will apply to everything else that we study about structure in this book. Without a desire to change, a vision, counting the cost, and a plan; you cannot make the needed adjustments so that God can send you His growth. The next step is to work on *you*. Let's make sure that you are structured for growth.

## chpt 4:
# STRUCTURING YOURSELF FOR GROWTH

In the rest of this book we will talk about different ways to evaluate if your ministry is structured for growth. We will talk about organizational structure, volunteer structure, and facilities. Before we tackle any of those, however, you must first evaluate yourself. You can work hard to get every structure set to grow, but if you personally are stuck in maintenance mode, that growth will overwhelm you.

Before God can send you great things, you have to be faithful in what you have. Matthew 25:23 says, "'Well done, good and faithful servant! You have been faithful with a few things; I will put you in charge of many things.'" You need to make sure you are managing the tasks God has given you, while at the same time figuring out how to expand your abilities to handle more.

There are areas of your personal life that need to be structured for growth. As we examine each area, ask yourself if you are structured for maintenance or for growth. If you feel that you are barely keeping your head above water, then that is probably a sign that you need to work to prepare for growth.

## SPIRITUAL LIFE

As believers, we know that our first priority should be developing our relationship with God. Unfortunately, there are times in ministry when you can get by with coasting spiritually. You can get by using just talent and natural ability. However, you can only do so much in your own power for so long. You will crash, and it will be ugly. Keep your own spiritual life real. Read your Bible. Pray. Worship. Go to church. If you don't make it a priority to attend service now, you won't do it when you have more kids in your ministry. Do not let your ministry replace your personal walk with Christ. Which spiritual disciplines do you need to work on so that God can grow YOU before He expands your ministry?

## PROTECT YOUR FAMILY

Way too many families have been sacrificed to the ministry. I always say that the greatest testimony of my ministry is what God does in my family. Lots of people can do my ministry work, but my girls only have one daddy. Anyone can do what I do for the church, but my wife only has one husband. If they aren't a priority now, I won't make them a priority when God sends growth to my ministry. Set up safeguards in your life that will protect you from any temptations that could devastate your family and your ministry. First Peter 5:8 tells us that the devil is like a roaring lion, seeking whom he may devour. He knows that if he can be successful in attacking your family, he can injure you, your family, and the church in one swoop. Don't let him. Make it a habit to regularly date your spouse and to invest in your kids. I never want to forget that God created the family before He created the church, so that's the order I try to follow too.

## TIME MANAGEMENT

I know what you are thinking; *I knew sooner or later Jim would have to say something about managing time.* Well, here it is. Time management systems keep you from being overwhelmed. If you have not read my book *Beat The Clock,* you should. Determine which tools you need to incorporate right now. If you feel like you have a good grasp on your schedule, that's great. But are you ready for more? Many people don't use calendars because they can keep up with appointments in their memory. That's great for them, but you can only remember so much. I use my brain for dreaming and planning and thinking. I use paper and my calendar for remembering. Even if you don't feel like you need tools or systems right now, get in the habit of using them, or take your habits to the next level so that you will be ready when the busyness hits.

## PRODUCTIVITY

To grow, you have to have some smart work and some hard work. Productivity really matters. It really matters how effective the things are that you do. If you aren't checking to make sure that you're getting results, you're not working smart. It's not enough to just write down how you want to spend your time; you've got to stop and look at how you really spent it. See if you spent it in a way that is really bearing fruit, or evaluate if you need to make some changes.

The ministry looks a whole lot like work. I have a lot of people who get onto me and tell me that I work too much. You know what? If you worked as much as me, you'd get as much done as I get done.

It's important that we work smart, but we also have to work hard. We have to have that whatever-it-takes mentality. This is a habit we never can get away from if we want to increase our abilities to handle more. It will cause us to stretch and grow and also see our dreams come true.

## HAVE AN OUTLET

Find a hobby that lets you focus your mind and energy for a while on something other than ministry. I love to go to guitar shows and to ride my bike. In recent months, I've even thrown photography into the mix. When you're busy, it is easy to say that you don't have time for the things that are restful. I have learned that sometimes when life is craziest is exactly when I need to get out of town to regroup. You also need safe people that you can talk freely to. (This is another benefit of being in a mentoring and coaching program like Infuse.) Ministry leadership can be a lonely place if you let it, so don't you let it.

## CONNECT WITH OTHER LEADERS

As your ministry grows, it is also becomes more and more beneficial to connect with as many other ministers as you can. It can be easy to remain in your own little world because you have so much to do. Yes, you are busy, and if God grows your ministry, you'll be even busier. Other churches have either faced similar problems as you, are facing them now, or will face them eventually. Networking opens your eyes to what others are doing and how they're solving problems. You can have people with like-minds to brainstorm with or vent to. One of the neat parts of my Infuse mentoring groups has been watching leaders from different denominations and different sized churches all over the country connect. These days networking is so easy with social media. Twitter™, Facebook™, and especially cmconnect.org are excellent resources for finding other kidmin people. You also need to pick up the phone and call other children's ministers in your area. Better yet, buy them lunch, and develop a professional friendship.

## PERSONAL GROWTH

Are you committed to being a growing leader? You should never be done growing and changing until you're dead. Be intentional about continuing to grow and stretch yourself. It is no one else's responsibility to make sure you grow but yours. God likely won't send growth to your ministry if your personal level is not ready to handle it. Growing leaders read and study. I read lots of blogs (you can see my blogroll on my Leader2Leader blog at jimwideman.com).

Growing leaders seek opportunities through conferences, coaching, or other resources. Before every conference, I make a list of the people I want to connect with and the questions I want to ask them. I have discovered that I can learn from anyone. *I also want to be intentional about what I am learning so that I have at hand the information, facts, and how-tos when it's time to implement them.*

Being a leader is not as hard as people make it out to be. It's simple to tell if you're good at leading: just look back and see how many people are following you. The more people following and growing in their leadership abilities, the greater your leadership level. You know you're a great leader when you see people following the people following you. When you up the leadership level of those around you, you move from being a good leader to a great leader.

# GROWING IN THE FUNCTIONS OF A LEADER

I define leaders by their ability to do the five traits used to describe leaders of God's people found in 1 Peter 5:2-4:

> Be shepherds of God's flock that is under your care, watching over them—not because you must, but because you are willing, as God wants you to be; not pursuing dishonest gain, but eager to serve; not lording it over those entrusted to you, but being examples to the flock. And when the Chief Shepherd appears, you will receive the crown of glory that will never fade away.

I've taught this a million times, so if you've followed a lot of my teaching, you might be tempted to skip this section. But it's always good to review. **The key to being a good leader is evaluating your leadership in all five of the following areas.** You want to make sure you are set up to grow in each of these areas as your ministry grows. You don't want to be stuck in a maintenance structure for any of these.

**I. FEEDER** - The *King James Version* of this passage says, "Feed the flock of God." Feeding is more than just your ability to teach. There's got to be training. The bigger the flock, the more people there are that need to be involved in the feeding process. Just like there's a big difference in cooking for your family and cooking for a banquet at a hotel; there's a lot more people involved when you're feeding a flock instead of just yourself. I don't know why churches hire a children's pastor, and then they think the pastor's supposed to do it all. No, as a children's pastor, you will have to train others to feed as well. You have to be ready to expand your methods of feeding as God sends you more kids and more workers.

**2. CAREGIVER** - I had the privilege of being the first children's minister in America to have electronic check-in. It started in Richmond, Virginia. I was speaking at a church and watching them check in children with a 3x5-card system. Bigger than life, the Lord spoke to my heart and said, "You need to do a better job checking in kids at your church." I proceeded to tell the Lord all the reasons that system would not work at my church. I don't know how you are, but I argue with Jesus a lot. I told Him that wouldn't work.

The next question was a question that still rocks my world today, "Why should I give you any more kids if you can't take care of the ones you have now?" Over the years I have been the poster child for children's security, but I don't use an electronic check-in for security purposes only. I have people at the doors for security. I have check-in systems to track and take care of folks. Without care and follow-up, you'll never be able to keep those you reach.

**3. OVERSEER** - This is one of the areas we don't do really well in in children's ministry. Years ago I realized I was more valuable to my pastor as a leader of leaders, overseer, and problem solver rather than just a teacher of kids. We will talk more about this in a later chapter, but for now, you should evaluate if you are personally ready to increase your ability to oversee your ministry, see things that need to be improved, and see what is being done well. Lead by thankfulness and appreciation. How will you do this when God expands your ministry? If you are presently doing all the work by yourself, you are not an overseer.

**4. SERVANT** - You gain those you serve. Jesus was a servant leader. He proved that He was someone worth following because of how He served. The same is true with the kids and leaders that you lead. You must serve them and those above you. Think about when your plate gets more full. How will you continue to serve your pastor? How will you resist the temptation to be more task-oriented and less people-oriented? How will you empower others to make sure that kids and volunteers are served?

**5. EXAMPLE** - Do you set the example for how you want your volunteers to lead? I determined long ago that I should make a list of what I wanted my kids and workers to be like and what I wanted their spiritual lives to look like, and then I set out to first make sure those things were in me.

To structure yourself for growth, you need to make sure you are personally ready to grow in all five of these areas. Make sure that there's not an area where you are just getting by, or a place where you are doing great but additional growth will quickly turn your ministry into a maintenance structure.

# THINGS YOU CAN DO NOW TO IMPROVE YOUR LEADERSHIP

Leadership is learned behavior just like everything else in your life. A lot of people say that they weren't born leaders. I wasn't either—I was born naked! Learning leadership is a process. Some things take time to do, but there are some changes you can make that will have a direct impact on your leadership. If you change your actions immediately, your levels of leadership and your outcomes are going to change immediately. There are things that if you'll start doing them now, people will notice, they'll see a change, and your influence over other people will increase.

## I. BE SOMEONE WORTH FOLLOWING.

You just have to work on you. Positional leadership is the lowest form of leadership anyone can have. So many times we try to lead by our function rather than our practice and example. Jesus practiced what He preached. He said, "Be holy for I am holy." (Lev. 11:44.) We also see that He knew the Word and did it. Those are still smart things to practice. He didn't act like there was a separate set of rules for Him.

A great question I like to ask myself on a regular basis is **has there ever been a time in my life when I was more in love with Jesus than I am right now?** If so, I need to repent and make some changes. I need to go back to praying more, studying my Bible, and being the person of God that I'm supposed to be. I'm the only one that can fix that.

It's important that you know the Word and actually do what it says. If you're going to be someone worth following, you should love the Lord, love the kids, love your workers, love your family, and love your pastor the way you want others to.

Practice and model how to flow with authority. Do you ever wonder why there's rebellion in your midst? Maybe you aren't flowing with authority yourself. Are you lining up with authority or are you sowing seeds of discord?

I often have children's ministry people call me to talk about whom they're mad at or who has hurt their feelings this week. Why do we hold grudges in ministry? Sometimes even people in the ministry act like they are back in junior high. I am not going to preach forgiveness to kids and then walk in unforgiveness myself. As a leader, I have to practice what I preach just like Jesus. You need to do a checkup from the neck up, and make sure your thoughts are lining up with the Word of God.

As I interact online, I am surprised by how many people seem to spend more time reading leadership books than reading their Bibles. Get in the Word, and I don't mean just to plan for children's church. Another good question to ask is how's my prayer life? When I look at the life of Jesus, I see He was a busy guy and had a ministry to the masses, but He always took time to pray. Do you wonder why you don't have the same results as Jesus? Most of us don't pray like Jesus.

## 2. SET THE EXAMPLE OF WHAT YOU WANT OTHERS TO DO.

Everyone who works for me is told when they're recruited or hired, "I've got some good news and some bad news for you. The good news is I'll never ask you to do something I wouldn't do. The bad news is I'm willing to do anything that's needed!" My mom has told me my whole life, "What's good for the goose is good for the gander," which is Alabaman for, "Set the example of what you want others to do."

Make sure you are following the same policies and procedures that you've set for your volunteers. If you have a dress code or a set time for arrival, then you need to set the example and do better than your volunteers. When I had a resource library, it would have been easy to walk around and give my requests, but I stood in line like everyone else. If you're behaving in a way that you wouldn't want every worker to model, then you need to change it.

Your attitude should also set the example. Sure, you're going to have bad days. We all have bad days, but people are watching your example. Paul was able to say, "Come follow me as I follow Christ" (1 Cor. 11:1). As leaders, that's our standard.

I believe this with all my heart: there may be people with more talent or ability, but no one has to outwork you. How do you do it? Here's my formula: dream, plan, build structure, create policy, and then teach, model, evaluate, and then keep repeating the process.

## 3. TAKE STEPS TO LEARN HOW TO GET MORE DONE.

We talked about this earlier, but I wouldn't be me if I didn't mention it again. Time management is the greatest asset of any leader. If you can become a student of time management, then you can get things done.

### *Here are five of the secrets I practice daily:*

**A.** Use the right tools. Every job gets easier when you use the right tools. What are the right tools to get more done? The first is a calendar. I use iCal™ on my laptop, my iPhone™ and my iPad™. I also use MobileMe™ to sync them. Second, I use a watch. You can't manage time if you don't know what time it is. In addition to my computer, I also use my iPhone™ to stay connected to others and to the Internet. I also use it for a timer. A new tool I rely on to stay connected is my MiFi™ Wi-Fi portable hotspot. I rely on all of these tools constantly.

**B.** Plan events that you need to do, and plan the steps for those events. I make appointments based on my priorities for everything that's important. Speaking of priorities, do you know yours? Are they up-to-date? I make appointments to exercise, to take my wife on dates, and to do the things I'm responsible for at church.

C. Break it down in to-dos. Remember if the Lord leads us in steps, we have to learn to think in steps in all we do.

D. Evaluate. Look at how you spend your time. Most people spend more time planning how they want to spend their time than evaluating how they really spend it. It's up to you to identify time wasters. Once you identify them, it's then up to you to do something about it. Years ago, I started evaluating my day before I went to bed. I also started using this time to plan how to make the next day better.

E. Delegate (i.e., use the time of others). At the end of the day, you only have twenty-four hours to work with. So after you've done these four other steps, teach them to others, and use some of their time as well.

People notice when you are getting more done, are more organized, and are using your time more efficiently. These practices will also get you promoted.

## 4. COMMUNICATE WELL.

You will immediately stand out if you return calls quickly or have someone do it for you. If it typically takes you days or even weeks to return calls, you can immediately make a difference in your leadership by returning them more promptly. Along the same lines, check e-mails regularly; or set a time to check and return e-mails.

Never do business in the hallway. People will stop me on my way back to my office, and I just have to tell them that I have to be sitting down. If I do have a conversation outside of my office, I follow up all conversations with an e-mail or memo to make sure we're on the same page.

## 5. SHOW UP A MINIMUM OF THIRTY MINUTES BEFORE EVERYONE ELSE and always have everything you need to do done before the first leader gets there.

This might not sound like a leadership principle, but it is. And listen, I don't like getting up early either—I'm an old hippie musician! But, if you want others to show up early, don't just set the example—knock it out of park. Being late is not the sign of a leader. I tell those I lead, "If you can't be on time, be early. Early is on time for a leader."

The best way to get others to come early is for you to get there earlier. Have it all set up ahead of time so you can speak to people as they come in. Let them know you love them and value them. Eventually someone's going to ask, "When do you get here?" or better yet, they will start showing up earlier to give you a hand. When I started going to my church over an hour earlier than I had been, I noticed my key volunteers started getting there earlier too. Then the people under them started getting there earlier as well. Appearances matter—they really do. When people show up and see how prepared you are to start the day, it sends a strong message about your vision.

## 6. LOOK YOUR BEST.

You might know by now that I live in a girl-world. I have a wife and two daughters. Yes, living with three women is like living with the fashion police. I love it when I'm ready to leave and head to church, and one of the Wideman girls will say, "You aren't going to wear that, are you?"

"No, sweetheart, I just put this on to see if you'd catch me before I left the house."

I travel a lot and meet a lot of children's ministry people. Can we be honest and say that some of us need a little update? Some of us need to get a little more current so that we can be relevant to the people we're ministering to. A great question to ask yourself is "What's your decade?" If you have the same hairstyle you had in high school, unless you just graduated, you need a makeover. Get some young people on board to see if you are stuck in a past decade.

Find people your age in magazines. For me, I like *Men's Health*. There are plenty of stylish people my age in both casual and dress clothes that I can learn from. One of my goals is to not dress like I'm going through a midlife crisis. In fact, a good rule to follow is when in doubt on how to dress, dress up. If you find yourself needing a fashion tune-up, have a makeover done by someone trendy. You might even know a stylist in your church. Another good tip is to find a good TLC™ television show like *What Not to Wear* or *10 Years Younger*; and study to show yourself approved.

I've also found that the more weight I lose, the more my leadership level rises. A leader is a leader, but at the same time you have to lead in all things. I think it speaks a lot about your leadership when you can make a disciplined change in yourself.

You may say that you're not going to worry about this because the people you interact with should not care whether or not your look is relevant. You may say that they should be more spiritual than that. But if you are not able to connect with someone, or you run people off just because you aren't willing to be someone they can relate to, then those people never will be spiritual either. Jesus came into our world, and it is important that we go into every man's world. If we're going to reach young people and tell them that the gospel still works today, then we need to package it in a way that looks like today. Packaging ourselves is a part of that as well.

## 7. START ADVERTISING EARLY.

If you would just start advertising a little earlier, you would see an increase in how many people respond. People don't come to church every week. In fact, I think every other week is the new "each week." So, if you really want everyone to hear what you're saying, you better start eight weeks out. Let your communication build each week until it's a really big deal. If you are serious about getting the word out to as many as possible, use more than one method. Don't put all your eggs in one basket. Use announcements, newsletters, postcards, and reminders. Use e-mails, evites, phone calls, or phone trees, websites, and even the church bulletin.

## 8. MAKE AN AGENDA AND PLAN FOR ALL MEETINGS.

A secret to getting your volunteers to come to your meetings and to keeping your staff from dreading them is to keep the meeting relevant. If someone doesn't need to hear the information that you are sharing, then don't invite him/her to the meeting. If your information can be communicated in a form other than a meeting, use it. I think sometimes we have a meeting just to see what meetings we need to have. ***Here are a few of my favorite meeting rules:***

    *A.* Select an ending time, and end on time!

    *B.* Use a timer. As I said before, this is another reason for you to buy an iPhone™.

    *C.* Put each item you have to share in order of importance so if you run out of time, it's the least important stuff that you don't get to.

    *D.* Stay on task. It's your meeting; act like it.

*E.* Stand up to talk. It will make a huge difference; plus, you burn more calories when you stand up.

*F.* Get feedback about how the meeting went from someone you can really trust. Always look for ways to improve yourself.

# 9. WATCH AND LISTEN TO YOURSELF TEACH AND LEAD MEETINGS.

Whenever you can, video yourself in different settings, and learn what you can. Listen to a recording of your meeting. I record every meeting I do, and I listen and try to see where I missed it and how I can improve. I also try to see what worked and try to duplicate that again.

Have someone take pictures of you in action. Seeing yourself the way others see you is always eye-opening.

Listen to your spouse. God gave him/her to be a partner with you. Listen to his/her advice, and do it!

Swap DVDs with another children's pastor and help each other improve. Some of the best relationships I have are with guys I've allowed to speak into my life.

# 10. CATCH PEOPLE DOING THINGS RIGHT.

Leading by encouragement is one of the most important things any of us can do. Each weekend at my church, I have every staff member turn in to me the names of at least three people they have caught doing something right. My staff also has to turn in to me the names of three people they sent thank-you notes to. Thank-you notes are huge. They are one of the best ways to lead by encouragement.

Brag on people publicly. When you talk to the leadership above you, tell them about people who are doing a great job. Don't just talk about the people who aren't doing what you want them to do. If you do, your superiors are going to get the picture that your ministry is full of unreliable people. Tell your leaders about the folks that are doing great stuff. Look all over your church, catch people doing things right, and celebrate them.

## II. DON'T DO THE SAME ACTION AND EXPECT THE SAME RESULTS.

Try different things on a regular basis. I love to find kids who have grown up and are serving the Lord. I ask them what made the difference as they were growing up in children's ministry. Lots of times it is something I totally forgot about, and I can implement it again with a new wrapper. Just don't keep doing the same old stuff.

Try different things on a regular basis. Sometimes just mixing up the order of your agenda will make a big difference. Add an accountability partner or coach, and have them sit in and critique the meetings you lead. Have that person come back, and evaluate if you're just doing the same things. What can you change so that you keep things fresh? It doesn't take leadership to change something that isn't working. It does take leadership to change something that is working well and make it even better.

As I've said, the first step to structuring your ministry for growth is to structure yourself to grow. But you know well that ministry cannot be all up to you. For too long, children's ministry has been a one-man show. Your next step as a leader is to enlarge the abilities of those around you.

## chpt 5:
# ENLARGING THE ABILITIES OF THOSE YOU LEAD

So far we've worked a lot on stretching you to be able to handle more growth. You are now ready to go to the next level. But even at your best, you can only do so much. God hasn't planned for you to do it alone. You need to continue to grow so that you can help those around you grow. Not only do you need to be structured for growth, but you also need to enlarge the abilities of your team.

I believe that leadership is something that can be learned. I know it can be learned because I am not the same leader I used to be. A lot of things have changed in my life—including the color of my hair and the amount of hair on my head! When I'm teaching, a lot of people say, "Man, I wish you could have taught me that twenty years ago." Well, I wish I could have taught *me* that twenty years ago too. I didn't always know these things, but I desired to learn and grow.

When I began growing as a minister, I started a quest in which I wanted to go from one level to the next. When I moved to Tulsa in

1990, I had experience working in churches about the same size as that one. But as my Tulsa church started growing, it was like nothing I had ever seen before.

That first year we grew 1,700 people in one year. I'll be honest with you; I didn't know what to do. There was one November, right after our Halloween-alternative event, where we grew 400 people and never lost them. That was great while we were in a rented facility where there was a lot of space to rent. But when we had rented everything there was to rent, suddenly it brought some other problems that I had never had before. I enjoyed finding solutions to those problems because that meant every week I was coming to work at the largest church I had ever worked for in my life.

Every church has problems. If you ever find a church that doesn't have any problems, don't join because you'll mess it up. You just need to find a set of problems you want to spend the rest of your life fixing. When I moved to Murfreesboro, I was excited to start solving a brand-new set of problems: World Outreach Church is a mega church in a small town. At the time I moved here, World Outreach had a smaller attendance than the church I had just come from, but it was nine times more effective in the community because it's in a town of only 100,000. I am so blessed to be faced with the opportunities before us here at WOC.

In the midst of problems, we all have a choice. We can either let the problem push us to grow and become a better leader, or we can just get stuck in the problems.

When I cleaned out my desk from my last Tulsa church, I found my original resume. As I was looking through it, I realized that on paper I was not qualified for the jobs I ended up doing at that church. Even though my resume looks pretty good right now, it didn't then. I had never had to recruit and train hundreds of work-ers. I had never pastored thousands of kids. I had never had a staff member other than a secretary. I had never managed multiple jobs at one time. I started in ministry before computers—we had a mim-eograph machine, and I made posters with press-on letters at my first church.

We all have to grow, including me. My abilities have enlarged; my staff's abilities and my volunteers' abilities have enlarged too. Senior pastors have continually come and hired my volunteers away. I used to think that was so mean, but now I understand what a blessing it is. It is up to you to either stay the same or enlarge yourself and commit to being the kind of person who is constantly enlarging others.

My growth began when I looked to the Word and realized my role as a leader had to change. In those early days of children's minis-try, people would hire a person to be the children's minister, and that person would have to do the singing, the teaching, everything. When I was first hired, I had to do the puppets, and I had to tell the jokes. I did it all. I just thought that was the way children's minis-ters did it. But as my churches started growing so much they needed to split classes and have other age groups, I learned that my job was not to do every piece of the ministry by myself. My job was to help enlarge those around me.

Ephesians 4:11-12 tells us, "It was he who gave some to be apostles, some to be prophets, some to be evangelists, and some to be pastors and teachers, to prepare God's people for works of ser-vice, so that the body of Christ may be built up." Pastors, or those representing the pastors, are not supposed to do all of the work of the ministry themselves. Our job is to prepare others and help grow their abilities. In 1 Peter 2:9, God tells us that His people are a royal priesthood. If all believers are priests, we are all to do the work of the ministry.

So if that is true, what do we do as the leaders of the ministry? If you have a title in the church other than apostle, prophet, evangelist, or teacher; then you come under the role of the pastor. You represent the pastor. The best New Testament word for pastor is *shepherd*. If you are a pastor, you are a shepherd. You know Jesus is the Great Shepherd, and the pastor is the shepherd of a local congregation. But every staff member, volunteer, and person in leadership is an under-shepherd. They represent the shepherd. The pastor of your church can't preach and change diapers in the nursery at the same time. He can't go and check if things are flowing smoothly and be an usher or parking-lot attendant at the same time that he's preaching. He has to have people represent him.

If you are representing a pastor, you are a shepherd. If you are a shepherd and you're helping a shepherd, I think it is important to know what the Bible says shepherds' helpers should be doing. In the last chapter, we identified the five functions that are mentioned in 1 Peter 5:2-3. In children's ministry, we usually do a pretty good job with the feeding and caring for our flocks. The function of overseer is what commonly gets overlooked. This is where we miss it. If you're doing all of the work in the area of ministry that you've been assigned, you are not an overseer. An overseer is a coach and a trainer, not just a worker but one who is free to see what is going on. (I told you before we'd be discussing this again.)

If you're reading this, I would guess that you struggle the most in being an overseer and doing too much. I believe God wants us to grow to be like a different model, Moses' father-in-law, Jethro.

Jethro was an excellent man; in fact his name literally means "excellence." Now if Mr. Excellence paid you a visit, would you listen to what he had to say?

This is what Moses had to decide. A man named Excellence comes to visit, and he could either let Mr. Excellence's advice go in one ear and out the other, or he could listen to what Mr. Excellence has to say. Moses' decision is even tougher since Mr. Excellence is his father-in-law. Here's the story. Moses' wife goes home to her daddy and takes the kids with her. This is a pretty bad sign for Moses, isn't it? His ministry is struggling, and apparently it is taking a toll on his family life. Things are not great, and later we find out it's because Moses needs to go to the next level in his leadership. He needs to stretch himself.

As we continue through the story of Jethro and Moses, I want to point out the ten steps it illustrates that will help you enlarge the ability of those you lead. These steps will also flip your team's switch so they can go to the next level too.

## Lesson 1:
## LEARN TO LISTEN.

> So Moses went out to meet his father-in-law and bowed down and kissed him. They greeted each other and then went into the tent. Moses told his father-in-law about everything the Lord had done to Pharaoh and the Egyptians for Israel's sake and about all the hardships they had met along the way and how the Lord had saved them.

*Jethro was delighted to hear about all the good things*
*the Lord had done for Israel in rescuing them from the*
*hand of the Egyptians. He said, "Praise be to the Lord,*
*who rescued you from the hand of the Egyptians and of*
*Pharaoh, and who rescued the people from the hand of*
*the Egyptians."*
**Exodus 18:7-10**

The first thing we learn from Mr. Excellence is to learn to be a listener. Excellence listens to all sides. Jethro had heard his daughter-in-law's side of the story, and then he comes and listens to Moses' side.

I learned very early in life that there's more than one side to a story. There are about thirty-six sides to every story in church work. You as a leader have to listen to them all. Who should you be listening to? Listen to the leaders above you. Listen to the staff and those you've trusted to help you. A lot of people have helpers, but don't let the helpers help them. Listen to anyone who has a pure heart and wants to help you. Listen to the parents in your ministry.

Years ago, what helped me the most was just listening to kids. One of my favorite parts of working with my puppet team was going to lunch in between the morning and afternoon practices. I loved getting them in the car on the way to lunch and just listening to them talk because it let me know how much God was really in them. I'd ask them, "What did you do last night?" and I listened. I listened to what they were listening to and what they were talking about. It was a way of taking their spiritual temperature and seeing if what we were teaching was really impacting their hearts. It was like what reading their Facebook™ pages is today.

An excellent leader learns how to listen to others. For Moses to be willing to grow and act in excellence, he had to be willing to listen to Mr. Excellence who was listening to him. If we are going to help others, we need to listen. Most of the great decisions I've made in my ministry have come from asking for help from other people and not making all the decisions myself.

Leader, you also have to listen to learn. Experience is the best teacher, but it doesn't have to be your experience that you learn from. Some folks come and talk about what is working, yet we get upset that neat things are happening for them and not for us. If you are going to go to another level, you need to learn to rejoice with those that have been blessed. Don't get jealous.

I listen to everybody. If I meet someone who has gone through a building program, I ask, "What would you do differently?" Sometimes knowing what not to do is as important as knowing what to do. It is important to ask. I want to rejoice with those who rejoice and mourn with those who mourn like the Bible tells me in Romans 12:15. Listen and learn however you can.

## Lesson 2:
## EVALUATE AND OBSERVE.

*The next day Moses took his seat to serve as judge for the people, and they stood around him from morning till evening. When his father-in-law saw all that Moses was doing for the people, he said, "What is this you are doing for the people? Why do you alone sit as judge, while all these people stand around you from morning till evening?"*

*Moses answered him, "Because the people come to me to seek God's will. Whenever they have a dispute, it is brought to me, and I decide between the parties and inform them of God's decrees and laws."*
**Exodus 18:13-16**

In other words, Moses said, "Well, I just sit here, and they come." I've heard it phrased this way in lots of churches: "Well, nobody else will do it." But that doesn't mean it is good! Other times we come up with other excuses like, "This is the way people did it before me," or "This is the way they did it when I was a kid—just one person running children's church." But those models aren't going to build fruit that lasts.

Jethro saw this because he evaluated and observed. Jethro was not willing to just take his daughter's word for it; he listened to Moses. But then he wasn't even willing to just take Moses' word for it. He watched what was happening for himself. I call that bearded-fat-boy management. I make a list and check it twice looking for who is naughty or nice. If they are naughty, I correct; and if they are nice, I send a thank-you note.

If on Sunday morning you make a list of things you want to do better, you have all week to fix them before the next Sunday. But one of the reasons we don't get to see and correct these things is that we are doing all of the work ourselves. We aren't being overseers. One of the best things you can do is use your MBWA (Management By Walking Around) degree. If you can walk down the hall and see more than hall, God has gifted you for leadership. I can walk through a hall and find at least thirty-six things that we can work on in that hall.

Jethro didn't just take the word of his family, and you can't just take the word of others either. My mama taught me a long time ago, "It is never as bad as you think it is. You are never as wonderful as you think you are. And when people tell you everybody is upset, count the *everybodys*." It's usually two old women that haven't been happy in thirty years. I don't believe reports just because they give them to me. I want to see it for myself. That's what Mr. Excellence did. You can't fix what you don't evaluate.

## Lesson 3:
## EVALUATE WHERE MINISTRY IS BEING DONE ALONE.

> Moses' father-in-law replied, "What you are doing is not good. You and these people who come to you will only wear yourselves out. The work is too heavy for you; you cannot handle it alone."
> **Exodus 18:17,18**

Have you ever felt worn out? It's probably because you're doing it alone. That's what Mr. Excellence said.

Evaluate areas where people are doing ministry alone. Remember what Jethro was seeing. He saw Moses doing ministry alone, and his response was, "What you're doing is not good for you, and it is not good for the people." Anywhere you don't see depth, you have a problem.

I have three favorite sports: high school football, college football, and professional football. I love football. One year I was watching Florida and Nebraska play for the national championship in the Sugar Bowl. I was cheering for the SEC, but Nebraska was beating them bigger than life. They had three fullbacks who were all walk-ons, and you couldn't tell who was in and who was out. They were beating the daylights out of those Florida boys. As I was watching the game with the Lord (because you know He loves college football), I heard Him speak to me: "You need the depth of Nebraska in your teaching staff."

I started realizing that anyone who wins dynasties has depth at all key positions. We need to build depth in our ministries. I know what you're thinking, "But no one can do it as well as me." I've got news for you. There was a day when you couldn't do it as well as you! Somebody let you sorry all over a group of kids and get better. You have to help people learn by doing. When I walk around churches today, I see some great things going on. But if you're forty-two points ahead, let that true freshman get some playing time. You are building for next year's team. You are building for that next service. You are building so that you can go to another campus. You are building so that you can plant another congregation. You are building for expansion. You've got to think this way to truly structure for growth.

Have you noticed that anytime a quarterback is not in the game, he is standing next to the coach and listening to everything he has to say? Why? Because he might have to step into the game and be the leader. I don't know why for years we've had assistants or back-ups just show up if they're needed to teach for an absent teacher. Let's put them in the classroom all the time and let them build relationships. Let them teach on assigned Sundays even when their lead teacher is there. Then they can be coached. Every assistant worship leader should lead once a month or every fifth Sunday. That way if they're ever called to go into the game, they have the experience to step up and do it.

I was one of those kids that used to play tricks on substitute teachers. One year our substitute was a neighbor of mine. My friends told me to act up, but I told them I couldn't because she knew my mama. When there is relationship and when others are used to the other person leading, the transition to hand off the baton is easier. Plus, duplication is good.

## Lesson 4:
# TEACH AND MODEL HOW TO LIVE.

> *"Listen now to me and I will give you some advice, and may God be with you. You must be the people's repre-sentative before God and bring their disputes to him. Teach them the decrees and laws, and show them the way to live and the duties they are to perform."*
> **Exodus 18:19,20**

It is important that we be people worth following. Why can we follow Jesus? He was worth following. We need to set an example in our walks with Christ, in the way we deal with others, and in our leadership. To be a leader worth following, we've got to show the right way to lead. We also have to constantly put into the next level of leadership under us. We should be spending more time with them than with everyone else.

## Lesson 5:
# TEACH AND MODEL PROCEDURES AND POLICIES.

*"Show them the way to live and the duties they are to perform."*
**Exodus 18:20**

Jethro points out that Moses needs to show them "the duties they are to perform." Every person that works with you wants to know two things: what do you want me to do, and how do you want me to do it? We'll talk in a later chapter about putting all of these types of things on paper and structuring them for growth. But here Jethro points out that you have to model for people how you want ministry to function.

The hard thing about multiple services is not necessarily finding workers. In fact, it can be easier because you are asking for a commitment *in addition to* church rather than a commitment *instead of* church. The hard part is getting multiple services moving in the same direction at the same time. The only way to do it is to have procedures and explain how you want them to do it. Make job descriptions, and write policies. Show people what these look like by modeling how you want them done.

Make sure you operate by your policies. Don't make exceptions on a regular basis. If there needs to be an exception all the time, then your policy isn't good—change your policy. I'm not married to anything but my wife. If there's a better way to do it, then let's do it the better way. It's up to you to know when you need to fish or when you need to cut bait.

## Lesson 6:
## QUALIFY WORKERS BY ABILITY.

*"But select capable men from all the people—men who fear God, trustworthy men who hate dishonest gain—and appoint them as officials over thousands, hundreds, fifties and tens."*
**Exodus 18:21**

People have different abilities and that's okay. You're not always stuck at your level of ability. How do you know if you're qualified to be a captain over hundreds or tens? Be a captain over a group of ten, and when your ten turns into twenty, you are on to something. If one of my leader's ten turns into twenty, I'm going to move him/her to another job, and I'm going to take them to other areas and give them opportunities to enlarge their abilities again. On the other hand, if your ten turns into five, you're not a captain of ten.

Your job is to help your people identify abilities and grow people from where they are. People have different gifts and abilities, and the happiest people I know are the people using their gifts and abilities for God. I grew up in a denomination where if you didn't know how to play a pipe organ, there wasn't a place for you in the music department. I was a young musician who idolized hippies and only wanted to play my guitar. They told me at church they couldn't use me, so I ended up in bars because the church didn't have a place for me. After I grew up, I purposed in my heart that in my ministry any young child who had a gift for music was not going to have to go to an ungodly place to use the God-given gift in him/her.

It is important that we purpose in our hearts to make room for the abilities and gifts that we need in our church. I think the farm system can work in more than just baseball. I think kids can grow up playing or serving in every ministry of the church until they are in the main auditorium.

## Lesson 7:
## IDENTIFY THE THINGS THAT ONLY YOU CAN DO, AND IDENTIFY WHAT OTHERS CAN DO FOR YOU.

> *"Have them serve as judges for the people at all times, but have them bring every difficult case to you; the simple cases they can decide themselves. That will make your load lighter, because they will share it with you. If you do this and God so commands, you will be able to stand the strain, and all these people will go home satisfied."*
> **Exodus 18:22,23**

Jethro did NOT tell Moses to go play more golf or take some more vacations. He told Moses to get other people to handle the simple things, but Moses was still to handle the hard things. Sometimes ministry looks a lot like work. In fact, it looks a whole lot like work most of the time!

What was Moses being taught in verses 22 and 23? Jethro basically told him, "Moses there are some things you can do, and there are things others can do. You've got to let the others do it." You've got to delegate the right things.

There is a stronghold that we have bought into in ministry. A stronghold can be defined as believing wrong information. There is a saying we all know by heart: the buck stops here. It means I'm the leader, so everything has to stop with and come to me. That's wrong thinking. There are lots of places the buck can stop before it ever even gets to you. If we acted like that in forest-fire fighting, we'd lose a lot of timber: "We could put it out now while it's small, but let the chief get it because the buck stops there." That's dumb. We delegate authority along with responsibility. We push authority down and allow people to represent us in small things.

Make a list of everything you're doing that someone else can do, and allow them to do it so it frees you up to do what only you can do. All believers can do ministry, so let them.

## Lesson 8:
# DON'T JUST LISTEN; DO WHAT NEEDS TO BE DONE.

> *Moses listened to his father-in-law and did everything he said.*
> **Exodus 18:24**

James 1:22-25 reminds us that just hearing God's Word does us no good if we walk away and don't do something different. Obedience is always the best. This is what I've learned: "Thus saith the seminar speaker" costs me a lot of money and heartache. *Thus saith the Lord* works every time. Every good seminar speaker was asked to speak because at some point in time they learned how to hear the voice of God, do exactly what He said, but then he/she took credit for it. It is important that we pray and then do exactly what the Lord is telling us. That's what Moses was told by Mr. Excellence. It is important to listen to the voice of wisdom. The voice of God and the voice of wisdom are always the same. Obedience always works.

## Lesson 9:
# PUSH AUTHORITY DOWN.

> *He chose capable men from all Israel and made them leaders of the people, officials over thousands, hundreds, fifties and tens. They served as judges for the people at all times. The difficult cases they brought to Moses, but the simple ones they decided themselves. Then Moses sent his father-in-law on his way, and Jethro returned to his own country.*
> **Exodus 18:25-27**

Moses let people help him, and he pushed authority down so that he didn't have to solve every problem. I worked at a church many years ago that I lovingly refer to as "Vietnam Assembly of God." It wasn't in Vietnam—it was in Alabama! But we constantly took the same hill and gave it back. We would fight a battle and win, at least I thought we won, and then we gave it back. For example, we'd debate whether we were we going to sing hymns or choruses. We would make one choice, and then someone would get mad so we'd change our minds. It was a frustrating time.

Ministry that is effective is willing to give authority to other people. Let those people represent the leaders, then follow through on their decisions. Don't take back what you've given to others. Responsibility without authority only brings frustration and never leaves fruit that remains. You must dare to trust people to represent you well.

How can you trust people to represent you? Put your heart in them first. Jesus modeled ministry before He turned his disciples loose. He let them ask questions. Can you imagine preaching all day in the hot sun without a PA system, and then just as you're about to sit down and rest, those closest to you say, "We didn't understand. What did you mean?" Not one time did Jesus ever say to them,

"Oh shutteth thou uppeth."

Jesus just answered their questions. He was committed to those folks, and He let them lead. He believed in those He was leading.

Push authority down if you're going to enlarge other people's abilities. Let them make decisions. If people come to you asking what to do and you keep instructing them, they will keep coming to you for the rest of their lives. The first time my youngest daughter went on a mission's trip, she came and asked me what she should do about something. I asked, "What would you do if you were in Peru?"

She said, "I'm not in Peru."

I told her I knew that but that I wanted her to decide as if she were. I told her to come to me with three solutions, and I would tell her which one I thought was best. We went through this process several times until one time I asked, "Which one of these solutions is Daddy going to pick?" She knew the answer.

What did I do? I taught her to think like me.

That concept can work just as well with the people I work with and the people I lead. By teaching them the process of coming to a good answer, you've taught them how to answer others and lead like you, even when you're not around.

## Lesson 10:
# NEVER STOP CHALLENGING OTHERS TO GROW.

The moment you get comfortable and let your people get comfortable is the moment you turn back into a maintenance structure. Constantly look for tasks of your own to give away. Don't let someone who is a captain of five stay a captain of five. Push to develop your people to enlarge themselves.

In this story from Scripture, Jethro must have lived happily ever after because we never hear about him again. So this story teaches us that Jethro came in to teach Moses how to do his ministry with excellence; we can do the same thing too. As you do these things we've talked about, you can have the leadership team you've dreamed about all of your life. You have to be committed to growing the abilities of your volunteers. Don't let people just show up and help you. Grow them into the dream team that you need them to be. That way you and your team can become all God has called your church to be.

*chpt 6:*

# STRUCTURING YOUR ORGANIZATION FOR GROWTH

We've talked about this earlier, but now let's imagine that this weekend over a hundred people walk up to you and say they want to serve in your ministry. I know you would feel like all of your prayers had been answered, but would you really be ready for all of those volunteers? Do you have a clear idea of what your needs are? Do you know what roles you could have them fill? Do you have a process for getting them in place? Are you able to communicate what you want them to do?

If you answered no to any of those questions, let me ask you one more. Could this be part of the reason God isn't sending you the large numbers of volunteers you are praying for? The Bible tells us He isn't going to give us more than we can handle. And He likely isn't going to entrust more volunteers and more kids to you if your organizational structure can't handle it.

Organizational structure is not just flowcharts. It's more than tiny boxes on paper. It is also policies, procedures, and forms. It is creating clarity so that everyone knows what you expect in order to facilitate the vision for the ministry that God has given you. Your paperwork, policies, and forms have everything to do with whether you are in a growth or a maintenance structure.

## TWO KEY PRINCIPLES FOR CREATING AN EFFECTIVE ORGANIZATIONAL STRUCTURE

PRINCIPLE 1: *If you do when you're small what you'll be forced to do when you're big, you'll get bigger.*

When I began working at Church on the Move, if you wanted a bus, you hollered out of your office door, "Is anyone using the bus Friday night?" If no one hollered back, you assumed (and the key word is *assumed*) that you could use the bus. It never had gas, it was never clean, and there was always someone else wanting to use the bus that happened to not be in the office when you hollered. It was a faulty system.

One of the proudest moments in my life came when I was packing my desk before I left Church on the Move. I decided after seventeen years I might need a copy of all of the forms I had created, so I filled out the form to request forms (that I had made, of course) and requested a copy of all of them. My assistant got the forms for me, and as I started looking at them, I saw one marked: "Last Revised 1993." I couldn't believe we were still using a form from 1993, but then I realized what it was. It was the bus form that I had created.

I remembered that frustration over the buses, and I remembered going to my pastor and saying, "I'd like to manage the vehicles." Did you know if you tell your pastor you want to run something, he's usually going to let you? So I sat down and thought, *If we had a whole fleet of buses, how would we have to run them?* In 1993, we came up with policies and procedures to run those two buses, In 2007, we had 100 vehicles, a full-time guy over the vehicles, three full-time mechanics, and another full-time person overseeing that whole department. And they were using the same form I had created when we had two vehicles.

As you establish your organizational structure, you can create a growth structure by asking, "What can we do now that we would be forced to do when we are double or triple our size?" If you seek to plan your organization only for what your needs are right now, you will be creating a maintenance structure.

## PRINCIPLE 2: *Everyone who represents you wants to know two things: what do you want me to do, and how do you want me to do it?*

People can't do what they don't know you expect. Every teacher, every coordinator, every superintendent, everyone who represents you, from the nursery window to the Sunday-school classroom wants to know what you want them to do and how you want them to do it. That's why job descriptions, policies, and procedures are a big part of being ready for growth. A smart leader also writes down the abilities needed for each position.

Why should people show up if you aren't able to tell them what you want them to do and how you want them to do it? Why should

Jesus send people to help if you aren't ready to do something with them? The purpose of establishing organizational structure is to answer these questions for your volunteers and to bring clarity to your ministry. Bottom line, not only do you have to identify where you'll put them, you have to identify how you want them to do the job.

## POLICIES AND PROCEDURES

The first thing you need to remember about creating policies and procedures is that you always do what is best for the people you minister to. I don't know why we try to do what's best for the workers and staff. I've found that when you do what's best for the group you are ministering to rather than doing what's easier on you, it is always best. Do what is best for the kids and families you serve. Like we said earlier in this book, you gain those you serve; when you serve kids and families, they are what you'll gain.

Make policies and procedures that are simple, clear, and easy to follow. I think sometimes in ministry we can make things too difficult. It's important that we look to simplify things on a regular basis. Things naturally get complex; you have to intentionally work on staying simple! It's just like your house: every now and then you have to have a yard sale to clear out the clutter. No one will read a hundred-page policy manual. Keep it simple. This is an ongoing process that will never end.

One of the advantages to my wife being a helper rather than a coordinator or a leader is that I am able to run things by her and let her read certain policies. She can tell me if they are easy to follow. Allowing someone else you trust to read through what you write or to listen to your ideas to make sure they are easy to follow will help you keep things simple.

Here are a few policies and procedures that you need to make sure you have in place, but also evaluate if they are contributing to a growth structure or a maintenance structure.

## APPROVING WORKERS

You are entrusting volunteers with the most precious people in your church—the kids! You need to have a clear process for making sure that safe people are in your classrooms. This means doctrinally safe as well as physically safe. This process should include an application, a background check, interviews, and reference checks. Remember early on to set up a process that will grow with you. Make sure the application works even when you have to process dozens each week. I'd be glad to send you via e-mail through www.jimwideman.com a copy of my current worker application.

It is amazing how many churches that need workers cannot approve them by reflex. If you need workers, you don't need a long system. You need to get them approved quickly. It shouldn't be simpler to get a car loan than to serve in your ministry. Look at how you can simplify the process so you can help shorten the time between yes and in the classroom. Limit the application to only the necessary information. Investigate the easiest methods for distributing the apps and collecting them.

## CHILD PROTECTION

Along the same line, you need policies that keep kids safe even after workers are approved and in the room. Unfortunately, the application process typically only deters creeps who have been caught. We still have to set up safety procedures inside the classroom environment that keep kids safe.

As you create policies that keep kids safe, here are some things to consider. Volunteers should never, ever be in a room alone. You should have a two-adult policy in place at all times. Determine acceptable volunteer-to-kids ratios. Be clear about how diapers should be changed and how bathroom assistance should be handled. Remember, your first priority should be protecting kids. The side benefit is that establishing and enforcing these policies will also protect volunteers from false accusations. When volunteers also feel protected from false allegations and liabilities, they are more likely to stick.

## CHILD ABUSE REPORTING

Your volunteers may be in positions where they may see evidence of abuse. You need to have a clear policy for how they should handle it. Who do you want them to go to with concerns? What is the line of authority for handling such a potentially explosive situation? Detail the process that will occur when abuse is suspected. You also need to know the laws for your state.

It is also very helpful to train your workers on what the signs of abuse look like. Bruises or random preschooler comments are common, but they can also cause concern. Help your workers by informing them and by giving them a clear next step if they are worried something above the norm is happening. This should be clearly stated in your orientation information for each and every worker.

## SANITATION AND HYGIENE

One of mamas' major fears for their babies is germs. You need good procedures to make sure that your environments are as clean as they can possibly be. Clarify who cleans toys and when. Identify which cleaning agents are approved. Train volunteers to keep babies from passing around slobbery toys. Establish procedures for labeling children's cups and other personal items to cut down on germ sharing.

Establish clear "Well-Child Policies" for parents so that they know if their kids are too sick to attend. This helps parents of both the sick baby and the well baby. Of course, like all policies, it does no good to have it if your workers aren't trained and given the authority to enforce it. Make sure your workers know exactly how they should diaper children and handle other bodily fluids.

Sanitation policies will help communicate that you care about babies' health, and that goes a long way to making parents feel comfortable.

## EMERGENCIES

Your team also needs to know what you want them to do in the event of an emergency. You need clear evacuation policies for fire and tornado. It's sad to have to consider it, but lots of churches these days also have procedures for locking down in case a dangerous person is on campus. You need to think through each of these situations, and explain it for volunteers so they, too, know what to do.

Another emergency situation that you need to be prepared for is what to do if a child goes missing. Who needs to be contacted? When and how do you lock down exits? At what point do you contact law enforcement authorities, and who is in charge of doing that?

Finally, detail what volunteers should do if a child gets hurt or sick. A procedure should be in place for how to contact parents and how to get medical help if needed. It is a good idea to document any accidents. You will need a procedure for that too! Follow-up goes a long way when an incident has taken place. A simple call to check on the child can go a long way. If a child has any mark on them when mom and dad pick them up, there should be an incident report that goes home with the child that explains what happened.

## FINDING SUBSTITUTES

All volunteers have weeks when they have to be out. It frustrates volunteers to not know how to find a substitute, and it can frustrate your organization when no one shows up. You need a clear process for this. If it is up to one person to find all the substitutes (and that person is probably you), you are in a maintenance structure. Like I said earlier, a growth structure can only exist when there is depth at all key positions. When this happens, having substitutes turns into a process that happens on its own, and it will take you out of the process altogether.

## CHECKING IN/CHECKING OUT KIDS

Check-in systems are an excellent example of doing when you're small what you'll be forced to do when you're big. In a smaller church, everyone knows everyone; so it is tempting to not have a secure system for checking kids in and out. However, visitors and new families don't know you, so having a system in place is reassuring to them that their child will be in good hands.

This definitely doesn't mean that you have to buy thousands of dollars of computerized check-in equipment. I made the choice not to implement computerized check-in at World Outreach Church. It didn't fit our culture, and we are doing fine with nametags. Most importantly, it is a system that can grow with us. You need to develop a system that safely gives the right kids to the right adults and that fits the culture of your church. Record keeping and follow-up is another part of the process that has to happen by reflex.

## RESOURCES

I worked at a church one time in Montgomery, Alabama, where everyone had their own glue, crayons, and pencils. It was an accounting nightmare. The Wednesday-night program had to have their own supplies, and the Sunday people had to have theirs. I remember looking at those people and saying, "Let's just buy in bulk. They're all *our* crayons." You would have thought I had asked for body parts. The whole idea was that we could check in, check out, and buy in bulk. Rather than buy more-expensive, individual Elmer's™ glues, we would buy glue by the cement truck, back it up, fill the bottles ourselves, and save money.

A clear system for handling resources will cut down on a lot of stress in your ministry. In war, one tactic of the enemy is to cut the supply lines. If you can make sure that your people have the stuff that they need to do the work of the ministry, you have won part of the battle.

Create an easy-to-understand system for buying, restocking, requesting, and replacing supplies. Clear lines of communication of how individual ministries share supplies will keep you out of the situation I was in.

## ROOM USAGE/SETUPS

In smaller churches, reserving space probably looks a lot like our original plan for reserving buses—finders' keepers! But this system will turn into a maintenance structure for your church. Systems for reserving rooms and getting them set up the way you want them will save a lot of headaches. Remember, go ahead and plan what you would if you had three or four times the number of rooms you have right now. Several church database systems now come with a module to handle room reservations so the process can all be online.

## CALENDAR

A big thinking change from a small church to a large church is switching from departmental calendaring to church-wide calendaring. It is important that you plan your ministry's year around the vision of your pastor and supplementing church-wide plans.

Take a look at your calendar and see if it lines up with the vision of the house and the church-wide plans. The goal is to build momentum corporately so that the family moves forward as a unit.

## FORMS

That bus form from 1993 was an oldie but a goodie. No matter how many vehicles they bought, they could still use that same form. It was part of a growth structure. Not many people get as excited about a good form as I do, but forms are key to your organizational structure. Many of your policies and procedures need a good form to help them be effective. And just like my bus form, they need to be able to grow with your ministry so that you are not constantly rewriting them.

Here are just a few of the forms that you might need to evaluate in your ministry:

- Visitor Registration forms
- Accident Report forms
- Room Request forms

- Resource Request forms
- Feedback or Evaluation forms
- Weekly Staff Reports

## FLOWCHARTS

A well-done flowchart will show you every single position that exists in your organization. It will detail who reports to whom, and it will visually illustrate how authority flows down.

When beginning to write a flowchart, the first thing you need to do is list every place you could use a worker. If workers were no problem, and if you had people coming out the wazoo, where would you put them? You also need to know the gifts and skill sets that are needed for each position. If you need to hear, you need an ear. If a nose shows up, you aren't going to put it on the side of your head. The missing link to a well-designed flowchart is to have qualified middle managers and coordinators in the right places. We'll talk more about this later.

## JOB DESCRIPTIONS

Every single position on your team needs a clear job description—even the positions that aren't filled yet. Job descriptions answer the question, what do you want me to do? When someone joins your team, you can immediately hand him/her a job description that can answer most questions and take away a lot of fears. There are some key components that every good job description needs.

*Purpose* - Provide a concise explanation of why the position exists. Remember to use this opportunity to cast vision for each position.

***Time Commitment*** - Be honest in detailing how much commitment is required for the position. Is it Sunday morning only? Are there expectations for during the week? Don't purposely underestimate the time the position will require to make it look more desirable to your recruit. That will just come back to bite you. You must be honest and give volunteers a clear understanding of what you need from them.

***Lines of Authority*** - Share who this position reports to and if any positions report to them.

***Requirements and Expectations*** - What are the minimum requirements for someone interested in serving in this role? Different jobs will have different requirements. A small-group leader needs to be a born-again believer, but a door greeter may not. Communicate here how long someone should be in your church before serving in this position. Identify any moral or lifestyle expectations that you have. Don't ever assume that people know what you expect. Put it in writing.

***Responsibilities*** - List exactly what you want the position to do. Be specific and comprehensive, but keep it simple. Identify the key tasks and list them in order of importance.

Real change in your ministry doesn't come from changes in programming. Real change and real growth result from establishing growth structures organizationally. It is not the most glamorous aspect of your job, but it is the part that can set you up for growth. And consistency will improve your ministry.

Is your organization structured for growth or maintenance? If you are stuck, dare to stretch.

*chpt 7:*
# STRUCTURING YOUR VOLUNTEERS FOR GROWTH

Without a doubt, the most valuable resources you have in ministry are people. Julie's daddy always told me, "I'm not in the electrical business: I'm in the people business." As a church leader, that is even truer of you. You are absolutely in the people business. We have talked about enlarging the abilities of those around you and stretching your thinking beyond doing a one-man children's ministry show. Now let's figure out what you need to do to implement a volunteer structure that is structured for growth.

## MAKE A STARTING PLACE FOR YOUR STRUCTURE

To create a growth structure for our volunteers, we start by categorizing all of the things we oversee. There are different ways to do this, but it is important to do it in a way that makes sense for your ministry and for creating your structure. You want to break all of your responsibilities down into manageable chunks. This is where

I use the rule of twelve from the Bible. Jesus began his ministry with twelve disciples, and I think He's a pretty good example to follow. Begin by determining no more than twelve ways to divide up your ministry.

The first time I did this was in my church in Montgomery. I looked at all of the ministries I was over: I was over the nursery, preschool, elementary, puppet team (back in the day it was just puppets, but today it's usually called the creative ministries team), clubs for boys, clubs for girls, Sunday school, and children's choir. I organized my volunteer structure based off of these categories. If I had more than twelve, something had to be combined or restructured simply because I don't feel I can oversee more than twelve direct reports in one area. Jesus didn't, so I won't either.

Another way to set up your structure is based on the functions of your ministry. This will look a lot different than structuring based on departments. In my current position as the associate pastor of Next Generation at World Outreach Church, I have the huge task of rebuilding our student ministry, and I'm trying a different structure. I've identified the key functions of our student ministry: spiritual formation and programming, student care/follow-up, student-leadership development/service, and adult-leader development. My structure is built off of those functions. Instead of having volunteers who are just recruited for high school, I recruit volunteers who love to follow up with students or who have a passion for the programming part of ministry. This is also the way I plan on staffing.

Keep in mind that direct-reports and the people we consider staff don't have to be paid. In Montgomery, every single one of those people who were my direct reports was a volunteer. I had a staff meeting with them once a month just like they were paid folks. I do not manage people that I pay or don't pay any differently. I let them know the things they need to know, and I always start with my twelve.

So, what works best in your church? What is the most natural way for you to divide up your ministry? Start there.

## IDENTIFY THE VOLUNTEER JOBS YOU NEED

Now that you have the basic foundation for your volunteer structure, your next task is to identify every single place where you could use a worker. If workers were no problem, what jobs would you have them do? Make a flowchart for each section of your ministry. I want you to get visual with this for two reasons. First, you are checking out what condition your volunteer structure is in. Second, you want people to understand the flow of authority. The Bible tells us that Jesus did not marvel at great healings or great miracles. The only time we know of that Jesus marveled was in response to a guy's understanding of authority. If Jesus is the same yesterday, today, and forever; then understanding authority will still get His attention. Teach people how to flow with those authorities. The flowchart will help them visualize how authority works in your volunteer structure.

Make sure you list every possible job. One way you can identify jobs is to identify things you are doing that someone else can do. You are not the only person in your ministry who can straighten chairs. You're not the only person who can check the wireless mic and put in batteries. There are so many things you do each week that others can do if you just give them a checklist. Have them follow that list, turn it into you, and then you're freed up to do what only you can do. Doing what only you can do is where you'll hear,

"Well done, my good and faithful servant."

It's important that all of us look for those things that we are doing and take others alongside of us to train them to do the same. I remember when my girls and I would set up our church's classrooms. On Saturday mornings, we would have lunch, and I would plan things like free-jeans Saturday for our time together. Then we'd all go up to the church and set up. One day it dawned on me that I could let them set up alone. I could check it after they finished, and that would give me time to do something else. It's the same principle with every volunteer. There are things you are doing that other people can do if you will let them. Take them with you, teach them what you know, inspect what they do, plug them in, and move on to something else! Training happens when we put into people and we don't release them until they know what we know.

Another key area that you need to address is middle management and leadership development. It is funny to me that I can tell a joke that is humorous anywhere. For example, what's yellow and sleeps six? A department of transportation vehicle. We've all seen one person with a shovel and five people standing around watching that person. When I drive by, I want to yell out the window, "Someone be the supervisor and tell everyone else to get a shovel."

Just think how many more potholes they could fix if everyone had a shovel. Middle management makes a huge difference in our structure because middle managers in the right places can tell worship leaders to check nametags as kids are leaving service, and then the lead teacher doesn't have to do it. They are handling details while you are able to walk around and do fat-bearded-boy management stuff—like I said before, making a list and checking it twice.

Find people doing good things, and send them a thank-you note.

Find people doing things wrong, and address that during the week. But this is a lot harder if you are the only one with a shovel.

# IDENTIFY THE RIGHT PEOPLE FOR THE JOBS

Next, chart where you have positions filled. Fill in the names of people who are currently serving. I actually start from the top down rather than from the bottom up. When I start looking at structure, I start with my twelve. This helps me know where I am with our volunteers. Sometimes we think we are in worse shape than we really are. That's why I put names in all of those boxes. The devil will tell us we don't have enough people, but we are usually not in as bad of shape as we think we are. Putting it on paper helps us see the truth. Sometimes when we have names in those boxes, we can see where we can steal from the rich and give to the poor and Robin-Hood them.

Your flowchart will also help you identify places where people can naturally do more than one job. For example, can your worship leaders also serve as your door people who check out kids? Are there people who are doing jobs that don't last the whole service that can field another job?

At the same time, you have to keep your people from getting overloaded. One of your jobs is to protect the sheep. If you err in any way, err on the side of protecting your sheep. There are times you have to watch out to see if the people you have given jobs to are being overwhelmed or if they are managing the tasks well. Burnout comes when you are overwhelmed for long periods of time. Have your workers lost the ability to put things into small segments? That is what overwhelmed means—losing the ability to break something large into smaller, manageable pieces. Suddenly, ministry feels like it is too much. When I look at my life and all of the things I have to lead, I don't look at it as one big thing. I look at it as different departments, different pieces.

You have to learn how to manage and look at those things in bites and portions. You cannot move a dead elephant all in one piece. That's where you've got to get a chainsaw. There are times in life when you just need to get out the chainsaw and start whopping some stuff into some smaller pieces. You're going to get overwhelmed and so are your volunteers. Anytime you lose your chainsaw, you're in trouble. I'm always on the lookout for people who I sense are overwhelmed.

As you look at the positions you need, identify the skills and giftings that are needed for each job. For success in the long run, you need to place people according to their giftings more than just filling an empty spot on your chart. First Corinthians 12:12 reminds us, "The body is a unit, though it is made up of many parts; and though all its parts are many, they form one body. So it is with Christ." You need to make sure you are not trying to put an eye in an ear spot, or a foot where a nose should be. God has made everyone with the gifts He wants them to use. Your job is to make sure you put them where they need to be.

There is a common mistake we make in kidmin. We take a great preschool teacher with a great class and make that person a coordinator. Now we have a sorry preschool class and a so-so administration. Over the years, I have learned to leave those great teachers in the class, put people around that they can teach, and find someone who is vocationally trained to manage. I will put them in the coordinator place, and then I teach them preschool rather than having to teach them management. It makes more sense to let them manage preschool rather than pull out the teacher and have a bad class.

Identify the people with potential you have around you. Notice that I didn't say just identify people who knock it out of the park and do it just like you. There was a time somebody saw potential in you and let that potential grow. It's your turn to return the favor. Ask yourself: what skills do they have now? What skills can be developed or need to be developed?

If you aim at nothing, you'll hit it every time. Find people that you can coach, and give them a goal. Are they the right fit in the right place to be able to do the right job?

Also, you need to look for people that are already in the organization, that have your heart, and that have the vision to move rather than just train up a new recruit. I want to know who is doing small things well. There were times that we would take over a new ministry, and I would tell some folks, "Hey, I need to move you into this area for a little while as we put the vision of our department in this area."

There's another important reason to ask, who is doing small things well? My Bible tells me that if you're faithful in small things, He will make you ruler over much. If I'm looking to promote someone, I want to look for someone who is already doing things well.

I recruit by vision, not by duty. I place people according to their gifting and abilities. **There are three things I want to know about the people in my church that help me:**

1. *What do you do for a living?* If you manage a rent-a-car company in seven different states, I believe you can manage the distribution of crayons. On the flip side, some of the surgeons in my church want to stand at the door and do nothing

because they don't want to think about anyone's pancreas. Our largest employer in the area is Nissan™, and I have a boy who can manage parts and gets parts manufactured for all Nissan dealerships. At our cookout, I put him over the distribution of hamburgers. He translates his vocation to ministry.

2. **What are your hobbies?** There are guys who want to justify purchases to their wives, and they will build anything you can think of. I can just hear them say, "Honey, I can't come in. I'm building this for Brother Jim and Jesus."

3. **What did you as a stay-at-home mom do before you were a mom?** There are a lot of people who are professionally trained as graphic artists, interior designers, lawyers, and more. They aren't currently using their degrees, but they may volunteer time. A good database could store this information about the people of your church.

When I think about volunteers, I want the people who are both gifted and fully committed, but I don't ever hesitate to ask someone to do something small for the kingdom as well. Every time you give someone an opportunity to commit is great, but you need to ask for a sacrifice every once in a while too. There are two types of volunteers: the pigs and the chickens. The pig is the big stuff for breakfast—you know; greater love has no one than whoever lays down his bacon and ham and sausage for a friend. The pig is the main player; the chicken is only a major contributor—he gets to live another day, but his sacrifice makes a difference as well. In your ministry there are people who will write newsletters or design e-mails or write HTML code, but they will never teach a class. Their contribution is important too. Don't overlook people who will help you excel by handing you an egg but not necessarily the bacon.

I had a guy on my church staff in Birmingham who was president of Barber's™ dairy. I told him, "I'll never ask you to work in children's ministry, but I want you to give me a hundred dollars anytime I ask for it."

He said, "Okay, that's worth it."

He would tell me that he didn't like to work with kids, but he could still help with money. That way it was a blessing for him and me. He sent everyone to camp who couldn't afford it, and he paid for stuff we needed. It was a tremendous blessing, and he never had to work with kids. We both won. He helped; he just did it by sacrifice rather than total commitment.

Here's one last thing that took me twenty years to figure out about getting the right people. Everyone I hired had to go through a probation period, but I never put that stipulation on my volunteers, so I started telling my volunteers that for thirty days they had to shadow someone else. I found out a lot about each volunteer during that time. Did they show up? Did they come on time? Did they enjoy what they were doing? At the end of the thirty days, I asked them if they thought the position fitted. If it didn't, I moved them to a place of success. Helping them be successful is more important than filling in my flowchart.

# KNOW YOUR TEAM

Know your team, and always be on the lookout for a new recruit or trade. If there's someone you have in the wrong slot, you need to let people on the front end know that you might move them.

How do you know your team? It's simple. Spend time with them. Discipleship is simply spending time with someone who is Christ-like in an area. When you spend time with others who are different, you let your Christ-likeness rub off. There's no way you can disciple your team if you aren't spending time with them. Spending time with the people you lead has to become a part of your lifestyle.

A lot of times in ministry, we spend time with the people who are least productive. It's not that we're going to forget about them and not minister to them. But if you spend your time with your most productive people, they will help you minister to the least productive.

There is an order to how I spend time with workers. I try to do it like Jesus did. Jesus had His twelve disciples, but the Bible tells us about many times that He spent extra time with just three: Peter, James, and John. Beyond that, John is referred to as "the disciple Jesus loved." So He had twelve, then three He invested more in, and then He was even closer to just one.

I spend time with the twelve who are my direct reports. Then, within the twelve, I start looking for three that I can put into, three that I feel can run things in my absence. Then out of those three, I start thinking about who could be my successor. Keep in mind, sometimes you put into somebody, and he/she makes choices that can disqualify him/her.

We want to spend individual time with the most productive people, but we also want to spend group time. This isn't an either/ or thing. Sometimes it is a both-at-the-same-time thing. You must look for ways to spend time with folks. Jesus didn't equally spend time with everyone. You must understand that at different times you are going to spend individual time with people that need it, and some people you will just spend time with in a group.

# BUILD DEPTH

The key to having a growth structure for volunteers is to build depth into your team. You've got to be deep. In football, you need a second and a third string. Why is children's ministry any different?

The way I started this was with that same flowchart. I added an assistant to every position. Now, lots of times we have assistants, and all they ever do is assist. What if you took those assistant teachers and told them that every fourth Sunday it was their turn to lead the class—with the lead teacher there to coach. What if you had an assistant worship leader who knew that on every fifth Sunday, he/she would be flying solo? I can hear you saying, "But they won't do as good of a job." Nope, and neither did you when someone gave you your first chance. But they get to learn. And one day, when your pastor announces that you are adding a service, or when your growth means you need to open new classrooms, you will already have people trained to step into those positions. Then you start over building depth again.

Look for any place in your structure where ministry is being done alone. That is a sign of a maintenance structure. To create a growth structure, you need to develop a strong second string. And when you're done with that, get busy on your third string.

# DEVELOP YOUR TEAM

Once you have your team in place, you are not done. If everyone stays at the same level where you started, you will quickly have a maintenance structure again. Your job is to keep them growing. Keep developing leaders so that you can keep promoting and bringing in fresh volunteers.

If you were one of my leaders, there's a great exercise I would do with you. First I would have you get out a piece of paper, write your name on it, and number it one through three. Then I'd instruct you to identify three things you could be doing better. I would then ask you to turn those into me, and I'd assign a deadline for you to have those things accomplished. We'd meet and make a plan to make those happen. Finally, I'd hold you accountable.

After a few weeks or a few months, all those would have been finished, so I'd have you get out another piece of paper. Then I'd ask you to write your name at the top, number it one through three, and repeat the process. This would force you to grow. You can do this with your leaders too. This process will help you know where your people are, and it will help them pull off more growth.

So, where do you start? How do you use all that you just learned to create your own volunteer growth structure? You can do it. Go now and put your dream structure on paper. Make sure you include depth. Go find the people, and always be on the lookout for ways to develop them. And remember; continuously evaluate your volunteer structure to prevent it from returning to a maintenance structure.

# chpt 8:
# STRUCTURING YOUR FACILITIES FOR GROWTH

Just because you want to grow, doesn't mean you will grow. If all it took were just wanting, we'd all be in mega churches. Growing is a biblical concept. Whenever my mama sees me, she thanks God that I was born small. That's God's plan—things start out small. The Bible tells us not to despise small beginnings, but it doesn't say we have to live there! If you had a child and that baby was the same size and weight at age sixteen as the day you brought him home from the hospital, I don't think you'd be waiting that long to call and ask the doctor what is wrong.

Our ministries are the same way. It is God's will that you grow. People often say that we don't live in the book of Numbers; we live in the book of Acts. That's true, but if you read the book of Acts, it has a lot of numbers. And if you look in the book of Acts, notice that every time you see a number and you keep reading a little bit, you find a bigger number. God really does want us to grow. I know I've said that a lot throughout the pages of this book, but I am not convinced that most people in ministry are convinced that it is God's will for their churches and ministries to grow.

A New Testament church is one that grows every day. The Bible says that God added to the church daily. Isaiah 54:2-3 teaches us something key about growth:

Enlarge the place of your tent, stretch your tent curtains wide, do not hold back; lengthen your cords, strengthen your stakes. For you will spread out to the right and to the left; your descendants will dispossess nations and settle in their desolate cities.

One component that you have to evaluate is your facility. Is your facility a growth structure or is it a maintenance structure? Are you prepared to fit more people or are you just maintaining your current attendance?

Sometimes I think we take facilities for granted. We want to grow, but it is important that we grow in our facilities and that our facilities have room. Families come as units. They don't come just as individual people. We can have room in the sanctuary but not in our children's spaces, and it could be stunting our growth. Just because we have room for more people in the sanctuary doesn't mean we can park more people in the parking lot or that we can fit more babies in the nursery. We could have a growth structure in one place but a maintenance structure in another. If we are falling behind in a certain area that is in maintenance mode rather than growth mode, we're not going to be able to grow.

I believe God wants our facilities to be able to handle growth just like our organization and our volunteers do.

# SEVEN AREAS OF YOUR FACILITY TO EVALUATE FOR MAINTENANCE MODE

## I. CLASSROOMS

Do you have enough classrooms? Do you have enough rooms in right ages? You aren't going to draw enough babies and young mothers if you only have one room for your nursery. Mamas don't want their newborns stepped on by the walkers. Assess every age group, and determine which groups could handle additional children and which groups could not. Make a growth plan for your classroom spaces. Decide ahead of time what your next step would be if you outgrew your current rooms. Evaluate other spaces that you could transform into kids' space.

Also make sure that you survey the size and safety of your rooms. A tiny closet may have sufficed for a nursery for a little while, but your nursery certainly can't grow in there. Make sure the rooms are attractive to parents. Identify any safety issues, and get them fixed as quickly as possible.

Take time to look at each classroom from the eyes of a parent, a child, and a visitor. Would you be excited to leave your child in that room? If you were a child, would you be excited to stay there? If you were a visitor, what would be your impression of the ministry when you saw that room?

## 2. HALLWAYS

Before a family even gets to a classroom, they have to get through your hallways! During the busiest points of a Sunday morning, how is the traffic flow in your hallways? Congestion frustrates people and adds extra confusion. You can't grow if your hallways can't handle additional crowds.

One of the best things I know to do for a crowded hallway is to look for a place where you can put the line inside the room instead of in the hallway. This quick-fix can cut down on the congestion, but it also gives parents a better view of the classroom environment and can also open up opportunities for better connection with parents at pick-up time.

Sometimes, to give your hallways a growth structure, you might need to make the hallway one-way. Directing the people-flow a little bit can help a lot.

## 3. BATHROOMS

I went to a church one time that just had one bathroom. There was one stall in the whole church, and it had to be used by men and women. The church people knew not to drink anything after midnight the night before. But that structure was really tough on visitors. There was always a really long line, and it seriously stunted the church's growth.

I will never forget the first time I went to a Willow Creek conference and they had turned many of the men's restrooms into ladies' rooms to facilitate the number of ladies at the convention. Even though I didn't like walking farther, I thought it was brilliant. They couldn't add plumbing for the event, but they were structured for growth. If your ratios are off, maybe you need to transform some men's rooms into ladies' rooms too.

Bathrooms are important! If bathrooms are stunting your growth, you may need to add a block somewhere. Get a plumber to evaluate how to add stalls to what you already have or to build a whole new set. Unfortunately there probably won't be an extremely cheap solution, but bathrooms are non-negotiable. While we're on the subject, anytime you have bathrooms nearby for little ones who are potty training, this is a win-win for parents, workers, and children alike.

## 4. SIGNAGE

If people can't find their way around, it is confusing. Signage is one of those things I don't think you can ever get enough of, but it is possible to have so many different signs that you confuse people too.

From every entrance, you should be able to find your way to every single classroom. It is ideal to have friendly greeters to escort people around, but you want to make sure that even if the greeters weren't there, the guests and members could find each area of the building easily.

Sometimes you have to move your signs from eye-level to someplace higher. If you hang them from the ceiling, people can see them as they move down the hallway. Make sure that you don't put "you are here" signs or anything else that causes people to stop and block the flow of traffic. Some of the same rules you use in highway traffic you have to use in hallways to make sure that people can flow throughout the building.

## 5. PARKING

Parking can also stunt your church's growth. You may have plenty of room inside, but if people cannot find a parking spot, they might just drive right out. Think about how annoyed you get when you can't find a spot at Wal-Mart™. That is not the feeling you want people to have before they even enter your building.

Evaluate if there are any alternative parking options such as grass or dirt areas around your property. Is there a place of business next door or across the street that might allow you to use their parking? Parking attendants can also help park people strategically so that guests can find spots more easily.

Once at one of my former churches, there was no way we could add any more parking. People had to park farther and farther away. We couldn't add parking, but we did add a shuttle. We at least let people know we were trying to serve them by keeping them from having to walk so far. When people know you are trying to do everything in your power to make things better and to serve them, they are going to be patient as you move from a short-term to a permanent long-term version of how to fix the problem.

## 6. FURNISHINGS

There's more to the building than just the room. Your furnishings must be ready to handle growth too. You have to have places to sit down and furnishings to be able to do the work of the ministry. Do you have the tables you need? If God sent you fifty new kids this Sunday, where would they sit? You might need to buy some chairs.

You may not even have room for chairs. A lot of people have gotten away from using them because they take up so much space. You might need to restructure and have kids sit on rugs on the floor. In my first church in Jackson, Mississippi, we ran out of space and built bleachers, which allowed us to accommodate a lot more kids. Recently, one of my friends from Infuse showed me Easy Risers™. They are little, easy pews for children's church, and I think that is a great idea. Just by adding those risers to one of our areas, we were able to seat more people. In every area of your church, look at what you can do to add furniture.

Also, evaluate your junk. It's amazing how much clutter we have in our churches. Anything that you aren't using or is just being stored, get rid of it. You can probably free up a lot of space just by cleaning out the stuff.

## 7. EQUIPMENT

Do you have the equipment that you need to take your ministry to the next level? You may really want a full band, but you don't even have a sound system. Or maybe your system won't accommodate all the channels you would need. Maybe you would like to incorporate video, but you don't have a decent projector. Make a list of what you need to be able to grow into your vision.

Ask if what you have is the best equipment for use and space. By adjusting or moving some of your equipment, you can clear off space where you can put more kids. For example, pick projectors up off of the floor and mount them from the ceiling, or mount TVs on the walls.

Come up with a growth structure and a plan to fix your current situation. Maybe your plan is not a long-range fix, but making things better on a short-term basis is a great first step.

In each of the seven areas above, ask yourself if you are in growth or maintenance mode (e.g., maybe your rooms are just fine, but your hallways are too small). Then come up with a plan to turn every single area into a growth structure. People follow people with a plan. Rather than do an overall plan, do specific plans for every area. Also, as you grow, keep in mind that some of those areas could quickly change back from a growth structure to a maintenance structure. You have to constantly evaluate your space and constantly think ahead.

# MAKING BIGGER CHANGES

Some people say, "If we could just build a new building or add a new parking lot, we would be fine." Did you know that it is hard to find a few extra million dollars lying around these days? Just building a new building or a parking lot may not be a possibility. It also may not be the right thing right now. God leads us in steps, and many times building a new building might not be a step; it might be a leap or a jump. You need to ask yourself what you can do to make room and create a growth structure in ways that are steps and not leaps or jumps.

## CAN YOU RENT OR LEASE?

There was a time when I was in Tulsa that we had outgrown all of our classrooms, and we were in a rented facility. It wasn't ideal to cut a hole in the back of the sanctuary, but it sure was great that there was more space that we could use. Sometimes you can use nearby space, even if it is something that you can bus to.

When I was in Birmingham, we had a Christian school down the road from the church. When we outgrew children's spaces at the main campus, we had parents drop kids off a mile down the road at another facility. This wasn't the best thing in the world because first-time visitors didn't know until they got to the main campus where the children were meeting. I always said that in children's ministry, we didn't have first-week visitors; we had second- and third-week visitors because it took them that long to figure out where their kids went. It wasn't ideal, but during this expanding stage in the life of our church, it helped us to have a growth structure.

## ARE THERE ANY TEMPORARY OR PORTABLE OPTIONS?

Modular or portable buildings are much more inexpensive than permanent buildings. These days they are also made of much better quality than they used to be. There may even be churches around you who aren't using theirs anymore.

In certain climates, you can get away with tents or some other outside setup. I've even heard of some folks using blow-up environments. That is common in Florida or California. We couldn't have done that in Oklahoma because it would have blown away.

## CAN YOU ADD SERVICES?

I love when my pastor says, "If folks show up at 3:30 on Tuesday, we'll have another service." It's a wonderful thing to work in a church that will do whatever it takes to touch people and expand the kingdom of God.

Adding services instantly increases the number of people you can accommodate without building anything. It is labor-intensive because you will have to build a whole new team, but adding services gives people more options—and people like options! Also, if you are moving from one service to two, it is possible that the quality of your children's ministry can increase almost instantly. It is likely that if you only have one service, you don't have weekly volunteers because they have to miss church all of the time. When you have multiple services, your volunteers can serve every single week and go to church too.

It is amazing that when we had just one Saturday service, it was the hardest thing in the world to get workers. Encouraging people to serve in one service and attend another one meant those Saturday folks had to make a two-day commitment. Not everyone wants to go to church for two days. When we were able to add a second

Saturday-night service, it was one of the greatest things that ever happened for volunteers. Everyone could treat it like Sunday: they served in one service and attended the other. It made a way for every worker to also attend church.

I have seen this work in two different churches. It also makes room to move or shift people out of the second Sunday service that is always crowded. At my current church, we just asked 700 people to move from our 10:30 A.M. Sunday service to our Saturday-night service during our New Year's series. We immediately filled those spaces on Sunday, and we also had the highest Saturday-evening attendance in the history of the church.

Some churches I know have dropped their second Saturday-night service because it is more work on the staff. I have found as we have said earlier that you gain those you serve, and as you serve your volunteers, you will gain volunteers. Here at World Outreach, our 7:00 P.M. Saturday service is the smallest of our four weekend services. We know that it is primarily a worker's service and a way to serve those in retail. But that is important to us, so we chose what's best for others; and God has blessed that big time.

## ADJUST YOUR PROGRAMMING

Sometimes your pastor and church may not be ready to add more services. While it may be helpful to you, it might not be the best step for the church as a whole. Another option is for you to change your programming.

It doesn't hurt a thing for you to change what you are doing for a time. Over the thirty-five years that I've been doing children's and youth ministry, I've had every kind of age groupings you could think of. Sometimes those groupings were because we needed workers. Sometimes they existed because that was just all the kids we had.

Many times we had to base our structure on our facilities.

In the early years of my time in Tulsa, we were growing so quickly that I would joke that all I wanted for Christmas was a two-story educational building. We didn't have a lot of places to have any breakout or small-group rooms, so we did primarily large-group ministry. We were growing so fast we needed every room we could possibly get our hands on.

Changing your programming from time to time may be a necessity to handle the growth. I know you might be saying, "I can't even imagine not doing small groups," or "I can't be a real children's minister if we don't do a large children's worship." You'll just have to do small groups in a creative way or at a different time. You may have to look for something to take the place of your children's worship for a little while. The important part is that you are sharing God's Word with kids. Your message doesn't change even though your methods might have to so that you can share that message with even more kids. A good way to stretch yourself is to always stay more committed to the message rather than a particular method, ministry, or program.

## CHANGE THE USE OF SPACE

There have been times my office had to be turned into a nursing mother's room—I didn't go in there! There are times at different services and because of the different crowds, that there may be different uses for rooms. You might have to trade out some rooms with another ministry to make sure you are getting the best usage out of the space.

You may need to look for creative uses for your own spaces. Can a small group meet in the resource room? Could that closet be transformed into a classroom? Is there a way to schedule your morning where multiple groups use the same room at different times? Could some kids be in small-group rooms while others are in large-group rooms, and then you switch? Dare to be open to think differently. If there is no one at your church that you can brainstorm with, make a phone appointment with someone you know or follow their blog and get them to brainstorm with you.

One of my best friends in the ministry is Roger Fields. I love his creativity and honesty. I also appreciate his friendship to me. I love to run things by Roger. In fact I texted him about this book, and he was the one who named it *Stretch*. I couldn't think of anything catchy or short enough to not fill the cover. I tweeted about wanting help, but I didn't like any of the ideas people came up with. In a matter of seconds, Roger fired back three title options that I could have used. Plus, I get to return the favor on a regular basis. Roger calls and says, "What do you think about this?"

Who is your brainstorming buddy? I highly recommend that you find one.

## START ANOTHER CAMPUS

Something that has really become popular in the past few years is starting a multi-site campus. I'll be real honest with you, to me multi-site opens up a whole other set of circumstances in children's ministry because it is hard to carry on the same program in the same way when you are in two different places with different leaders at the same time.

If your church is going multi-site, the first thing you have to do is determine how the DNA of your children's ministry can transfer to another campus. What can you do now to make sure that your ministry can be replicated?

You will have to be the voice for what kids need when space is being determined for another campus. Keep safety as a number-one priority. Also make sure that the space can easily accommodate the programming you offer. As with any new space, there will be things that you have to compromise on. Begin now by determining what is non-negotiable.

One of the things I like about our church is that we are a multi-venue or multi-site church on one campus. While our sanctuaries are multi-site, our classrooms are not. That is an interesting twist. I want you to see that there is no limit to an alternative, but you do have to think differently.

## BUILD A BUILDING

Planning a building can be one of the most stressful things you can ever do in ministry. That is usually a class that they leave out of Bible school and seminary. No one trained me to look at blueprints and speak architect language.

How do you know how much to build? One of the things I've seen over the years is that churches usually have percentages that stay the same. A church's percentage of nursery to adult, elementary to adult, etc. stays the same throughout the history of the church. The percentages stay the same, even as the numbers change. Twenty percent of a hundred people is a whole lot different than 20 percent of 1,000 people, but it is still 20 percent. Churches have personali-ties just like people. Some churches have a higher percentage of a certain age group, and that will stay consistent over many years though it may fluctuate a little here and there.

When planning a new auditorium, keep in mind that if you're looking to build something 25 percent bigger for adults, it is important that you convert what that 25 percent more means in your ratio of adults to each age group. Make sure you're increasing in those age groups too. I've seen churches build and actually decrease their space for kids because they didn't plan for equal amounts of growth. As a result, their old spaces were more of a growth structure than their new space!

When we built here at World Outreach church, we knew we were building a growth structure. We wanted space that didn't just accommodate the one sanctuary that we were adding. We were anticipating having three to four sanctuaries at the same time. I came up with what children's ministry space we would need to be 75-80 percent full in all four sanctuaries. That was the first time in a long time we'd had extra classrooms.

You know what? Ever since then, each week we keep opening new classrooms. This past January during our New Years' series, we had the largest weekend attendance our campus has ever had. We were 200 people short of hitting 11,000. The good news is we still have rooms to grow in for every age group from the youngest to the oldest. There will be a time when that growth structure becomes a maintenance structure, and then we will have to ask ourselves what we will do next: build, add on, or start another service?

When it comes to facilities, you can't throw out a new building whenever you want one, but that doesn't mean you have to be stuck in a maintenance structure. So many times we are just more comfortable with old problems than with new solutions. Take some time to brainstorm with some folks, and play a good ole game of What If? See what in the world you can do to come up with some alternatives to facilitate growth. *Dare to stretch!*

*chpt 9:*

# COMMUNICATING YOUR STRUCTURE

Once you've determined how you want the structure of your ministry to look, you still have a big job in front of you. To implement your structure, you have to communicate it to your staff, your team, and your whole church.

Communication is a challenge everywhere, but folks can't flourish if you don't know how to communicate your vision. Communication doesn't just happen on its own. Some people think communication is a by-product of going through the motions and just doing the things we do. I want you to understand that it is a whole lot of hard work. If you aren't intentional about making communication happen, it is not going to happen.

Think about the telephone. We take it for granted, but somebody had to go out in the woods, chop down a tree, knock off all of the limbs and bark, drag it out of the woods, paint it, dig a hole, plant that sucker, and then repeat that process several million times. Then they had to stretch wire from one pole to the other, and then the connected poles had to have wires run to the houses. From there, the right telephone had to be paired with the right jack, and it all had to be plugged in so that you could talk.

Cell phones require even more money, work, and brainpower. Think about the space program and the billions of dollars that have been spent so that we can say, "Can you hear me now?" We send e-mails and never stop to think about how the Internet works. The communication that you use with those you lead has to be just as intentional, just as on target, and it has to be the by-product of a whole lot of work. You must think intentionally about communication.

Not only must you intentionally think about communication, you must think innovatively. Innovative thought looks at different ways to do things. When you think this way, you look for ideas that are more effective. On top of that, we must continuously seek to have improving thought. Looking to make things better has to become a way of life. Communication also requires intelligent thought. You've got to think sharper, think bigger, and think more differently than you ever have before. You can't keep going around the mountain the same way you have before and think you're going to have a different result. We must understand that intelligent thought, innovative thought, and improving thought will make intentional thought a reality.

Communication has a high price. It costs a lot to put a satellite in orbit; similarly, there will also be a high cost for you as you communicate. It may not be a cost that you can count with nickels and dimes, but there is an investment you make when you choose to intentionally communicate with people. It is an investment that has a wonderful, wonderful benefit.

There are risks in communication: you are showing what you know and what you don't know. There is also always a risk factor of how what you are communicating is going to be received. Sometimes just one method of communication isn't going to get the message to everyone.

There is also a monetary cost in communication. There are tools and equipment and supplies that involve a physical cost. But anything that is spent to help share your vision and to help people do a better job at what God is calling them to do is a good cost. Just because it costs money doesn't mean that it is bad. As a matter of fact, it is good to spend money on things that produce great fruit. I hear people say all the time that they can't afford a Mac™, an iPad™, or an iPhone™. I can't afford to not have them. I have to have the best tools to do the work I have to do.

For example, the other day my recording interface broke, so I had to buy another one. Then I realized because of my intense schedule, I really needed a back-up interface just in case. The tools and things that are necessary for constant communication in all I do are priceless to me, so a monetary cost is worth it.

## COMMUNICATING WITH THOSE ABOVE YOU

The most important group that we have to communicate with is our direct leadership. I always start by communicating up. I align my vision and the vision I'm trying to communicate with the vision of the leader. I know you might say, "Well, I'm the children's minister, I should be the only one dictating the vision for the children." Remember, darling, the only reason you have a job is because you represent your pastor. The reason you exist is because your leader can't be in every place at one time. Yes, you are the central flow of where the vision happens for your ministry, but it is essential that you sound off to your pastor and to your leader and let them know, "This is what I was thinking. Is that what you were thinking too?" The place to start is realizing that anything that is a change of direction or a change of purpose needs to first be discussed with your leader.

I have found myself dealing with decisions that others made without giving me a say-so in them. It's not that I want to be a micromanager; I just want to help my team succeed. But if I don't have a say-so, they may fall flat on their faces, or we may have to go through a re-do. The same thing is true when I go to my leader. He wants me to succeed. He wants to make sure that I have thought it through and that my plan is the best thing we can possibly do for the vision of the house.

## COMMUNICATING WITH YOUR TEAM

Next, you are going to have to communicate to your team before you communicate to the general public. Where did I get that idea? From Jesus! He communicated and built a team long before He launched a public ministry.

One consistent tool to use in communicating with your team is staff meetings. Remember, *staff* doesn't have to mean paid people. Right now, I do my staff meetings biweekly. I do children's ministry staff meeting on one week, and the next week I have a student-ministry staff meeting. During those meetings, I go over group events and assignments that everyone needs to know. I let people individually communicate anything they need clarification or approvals on.

At the same time, I ask all of my staff to turn in weekly reports. Anything I can handle before the meeting, I do. If I can answer something ahead of time, I will. This cuts the meeting shorter, and they don't have to wait on me. Not everything has to be addressed at the meeting. These reports may even show things that need to be added to the agenda. If they have questions for me, they can e-mail in between meetings, or they can set up an appointment. Staff meetings don't take the place of individual meetings.

Anytime that I'm going to have a meeting with more than one person, I print the agenda. It is my meeting, and I get to set the agenda of what we're going to talk about. If there is something someone needs on the agenda, he/she must communicate it ahead of time. Again, as leaders we are communicating where we want to go and how we want to get there, so I have to be intentional. That's why that agenda is so important.

Another way I communicate with my team is through power lunches. I like to take my team out to lunches that aren't just about good food but about being productive over the lunch hour. I encourage my team to all ride in the same car so that I can set the tone and establish that there is a purpose to this lunch. I try to focus all the conversation both on the way there and during the lunch. On the way back, I wrap up assignments so that everyone knows what they can accomplish at the end of that lunch.

## COMMUNICATING WITH KEY VOLUNTEERS

I communicate with key volunteers in two different ways. In Tulsa, I did a lot of leadership lunches. At World Outreach, I mainly do team-leader meetings every other month. These events have been some of the best meetings I've ever been a part of. If I had to pick between general-worker events and these leader events, I would pick the leadership events. Spending time with the level of leadership closest to you is important. I communicate where we are going so that they can pass that on to other folks. This way we are all moving in the same direction. I also want them to see where we are now. I want them to hear my heart. This is a time when I'll teach a skill set. This is where a lot of my early Club lessons came from. Folks just don't have your heart if you don't teach them the things that are in your heart.

I can better tell where people are individually by meeting with them in a group than I can meet them one-on-one. When people are with you one-on-one, it is easy for them to go along and paint a picture that they are on board with you. What I love about doing things in a group is I can really watch what's going on.

In a meeting, there are two things every leader needs to do. Leaders don't just present the information; they need to watch, and they need to listen. Watch body language. Watch how people are responding to what you're saying. Listen to their questions. Listen for what they aren't saying.

Always be available before and after each individual meeting for questions. Jesus was never too busy for Peter's dumb questions, so it is important to let your people ask questions for clarification. It's the only way your workers are going to fully grasp your vision. Many times those people won't ask for clarification in a group because they are afraid they won't look good. So I come early, and after everybody leaves, I stay late to field those questions.

The problem that I see with meetings is that everyone tries to communicate to everyone at the same time. Well, there may only be so much time, but that is why it's important to let your key leadership help you communicate. There's a military term that would be helpful to use in the church world: *need to know*. If they don't need to know it, don't have them in that meeting. If you have a worker who has helped you for several years, they don't want to hear how to call roll for the forty-eighth time. Sure, you may have to go over that, but have a meeting only for those who have been serving six months or less where you can go over those things.

## COMMUNICATING WITH OTHER VOLUNTEERS

Let everyone that you meet with know that it is their responsibility to communicate with the rest of the volunteers. Remember, I want to push authority down every chance I get and let those leaders communicate. Not personally knowing all the kids or, now, all the volunteers used to bother me. But you know what? I know someone does. I can't communicate my heart with every single volunteer. It is our leaders' responsibility to communicate. The whole reason that I'm meeting with leaders is to equip them to communicate. NASA isn't made up of one or two people; it's a whole team of smart folks. The same thing has to happen in your ministry.

Sometimes you can use people's talkativeness to your advantage. When I lived in Tulsa, I had a chiropractor that loved to talk. He was a good man; he just liked to tell whatever he knew to everyone he knew. The good thing about him was that he would tell it exactly like you told it to him. He wouldn't slant it any way. So I would go to him and tell him when I was going to change something, and I would say, "Do not tell anybody." This good old boy would then tell most of my church, "Did you hear what Brother Jim is about to do with the kids?" He was actually helping because by the time I announced what I was going to do, 700 people were already on board.

Meetings with volunteers are necessary. At my church, we now do tri-annuals. All the workers come three times a year for meetings. Two of them are informational, and one is an orientation. We also do an appreciation banquet. Our volunteers come to these four events during the year, and we give them the dates at the beginning of their commitment. I use these meetings to share vision, inspiration, encouragement, information, and action. There's always going to be a need for meetings, but there's also always going to be people who don't come.

One thing we've started doing for the most important meetings is offering them at two different times so that volunteers can pick which time is best for their schedules. That helps busy families. We also look for times when our volunteers are already at church, rather than making them come back. Also, we utilize technology such as video trainings or podcasts.

## GETTING FEEDBACK

It also helps to periodically do a questionnaire. Rather than just give out information all the time, sometimes you need feedback. Remember that communication is a two-way street. So many times we do all the talking, and then we call that communication. Sometimes you need to do some listening, you need to do some evaluating, and you need to do some testing. You need to see if people are really grasping and doing what is needed to do to make the vision a reality. Otherwise you just running off and leaving everyone.

One great way to see what is happening is to go visit classrooms or observe them in action. I love to watch what people are doing and to see if they really understand what the vision is all about. It gives me an opportunity to show them how to do things better. Also, I need to make sure I'm catching them doing things right. I don't want all my communication to be negative. I want to communicate, "Man, I appreciate the things that you're doing and the steps you're taking.

We are getting so much closer to where God wants us to go."

Take your leaders to conferences or other training events with you. I love to make others' events my own by letting people know what I want them to see. Sometimes the things we were able to talk about beforehand or after are more valuable than the information we gain during the event. Sometimes I want to expose them to a different or a bigger vision. Any opportunity that I have to point someone to a bigger way of thinking is important and makes a big difference. If you can show it, it is much more effective than trying to describe it on your own.

## COMMUNICATING TO THE REST OF THE CHURCH

I use just about anything to communicate and pass on the vision. I'll use fliers, calendars, schedules, newsletters, websites, and e-mail blasts. One of the things I think we'll see in the next few years in every church will be a worker webpage. In coming years, workers will be able to download everything they need for ministry, from forms and reports to multimedia files and curriculum.

Even now, leaders can write blogs where they talk about all kinds of things their workers need to know. I know not everyone is web-savvy, but there are easy templates and inexpensive tools to make this happen. Don't run away from it. Your job is to lead people where they need to be. We want to be a culture-current church, and we want to help people move in the directions they need to move.

Make a good website for your ministry. It is a never-ending process as information and technology is constantly changing, but make sure that the information and look is current. Go after a look that fits the age of those you lead. People will often go to your website first before they ever step foot in your church, so make sure it makes a good impression. The better your website is, the more you can depend on it for communicating vision and information. Even when you use brochures, have the brochure drive them to the website. I am now making smaller publications than I ever have before, and instead I'm driving people to the information on the website.

Every time you have an event, you need to be getting pictures. You can use those in presentations and in video. Now with Flip™ cameras and iPhones™, there's no reason why you can't make simple videos showing what God is doing. Every place I can put a picture on a video screen or a monitor, I do it. A picture is worth a thousand words, and it is a great way to communicate a vision. Rather than show a picture of someone playing in a classroom, use a picture where they are worshiping God, praying intently, or responding to God. Those are the things that impart a Holy Ghost vision that is going on in that classroom. Those pictures convey the message that if you aren't helping, you are missing out on what God is doing in the lives of the next generation.

Also, every publication that your ministry can possibly be represented in, you need to be in them. It communicates that there are great things happening, and it communicates the vision. Are there women's ministry or men's ministry newsletters? Adult, small-group informational pieces? Share the vision of your ministry in each of these as often as you can.

Another thing that has been valuable to me is a phone tree. I can make one phone call that reaches all of my volunteers reminding them of what they need to do. I also use Facebook™ the same way. Make a group for your volunteers, or use your personal page. I post reminders on my Facebook™ for meetings, and I always have someone say, "Man, I forgot about that meeting until I saw it on your Facebook™." You can also use Facebook™ to share exciting moments that happen in your ministry, key points about what kids are learning, and other glimpses of vision.

I also use the spoken word. I constantly tell my pastor what God is doing. I've found out something about senior pastors. They're going to help you spread the word about the good things that are happening. Every time I have the chance to be in front of people, I talk about fruit. I talk about what God is doing. Whenever you have the opportunity, talk about the God stories and tell the good that is happening. Don't just talk about what's not happening or what you need. Talk about what God is doing. Encourage your workers to do the same. When you get workers spreading the news, it makes a difference.

Work on room décor, and make your venues the most wonderful places they can possibly be. When you are improving your structure and casting new vision, these types of changes can add to the momentum and excitement. There are things you can do on a low budget that can make a quick impact. You can also make changes in steps. Do small things that your parents, kids, and volunteers will notice.

We've discussed lots of different ways to communicate. Which one of these should you do? Do them all! Variety is good. That is true in advertising, and it is true in communication. I want to use as many different ways as I possibly can. As you work on these things and communicate to every group, it will cause your ministry to seize the vision and be able to accomplish what God has called you to do.

Start a list: which of these things do you need to do? What do you need to do differently? Read this chapter one more time, and look for ways that you can better communicate. As you start taking steps and communicating your game plan better, it will build your strategy.

Remember, don't try to accomplish too much too fast. Ask God for wisdom to know how far, how fast, how much is too much and what's the right amount.

## chpt 10:
# QUESTIONS TO ASK YOURSELF

You've read a lot of information in this book, and now what you do with it is up to you. Before you put this book on your shelf, let me challenge you to ask yourself a few questions. Take some time to pray through these and be honest with yourself.

## Question 1:
# HAVE YOU ESTABLISHED THE RIGHT STRUCTURE FOR WHAT GOD WANTS YOU TO BUILD?

Evaluate to see if your structure will support your pastor's vision for your church and your vision for your ministry. Make sure that you have a clear understanding of both visions. Start making a list of which parts of your structure have to change to accomplish the vision. Do you have the right people on board? Do you have things organized? Do you have the right space?

## Question 2:

# IS YOUR STRUCTURE A GROWTH STRUCTURE OR A MAINTENANCE STRUCTURE?

This question has been the recurring theme of this book, but it is critical. Does the structure you have only get you through until the next Sunday, or is it setting you up for the future? Be honest. Remember that your goal is to have every piece of your structure in growth mode. This will be a process, and it will take constant assessment. You will have to be on a constant mission to keep your structure in growth mode.

## Question 3:

# IS YOUR STRUCTURE SIMPLE TO FOLLOW?

Does your structure make sense to anyone but you? To help people help you accomplish your vision, you have to make sure that it is extremely clear. Fight for clarity. If it is too complex, it is automatically a maintenance structure. Structure is a tool to make ministry more effective. It isn't helpful if you and your people have to spend all your time interpreting the structure.

## Question 4:

# ARE YOU COMMITTED TO DOING WHATEVER IT TAKES?

You are going to have to do things you've never done before if you want results you've never had before. How committed are you to growing? Are you willing to change what you are doing now? Change is hard, but it is often necessary. If you are too tied to your current ways of doing things, you probably aren't ready to structure for growth. Are you willing to try new things and jump way out of your comfort zone?

You also have to be committed to some tough work. These types of changes won't happen overnight. You have a lot of detail work ahead of you, such as writing job descriptions and policies. You have a lot of vision casting and communicating to do. You have a lot of planning to do. Most of all, you have a lot of leading to do. Are you all in? Are you committed?

## Question 5:
## WHAT ARE YOU WAITING FOR?

I hope you're excited. I hope as you've read this book, God has given you a clearer vision of what the future could look like for your ministry. Even more than that, I hope He's shown you some specific areas where you can upgrade your ministry to a growth structure. Now is the time to get organized.

If you are like me, lots of times I will finish a book, put it on the shelf, and forget about it a few days later. If God has shown you things you need to do, don't put those ideas on a shelf. Commit yourself to the Lord to seek the very best, and work your very hardest to accomplish His vision. There are kids who need to hear the good news of who Jesus is. There are workers that need a place to use the gifts God gave them. There is a community that needs God's love.

So what are you waiting for? Get your action plan together and get moving. Now is the time for you, your ministry, and your church to stretch.

# LOOKING FOR MORE INFORMATION ABOUT JIM WIDEMAN`S INFUSE COACHING PROGRAM?

Log on to **www.jimwideman.com**
and click on the infuse tab!

---

## FOR A LIST OF OTHER BOOKS AND PRACTICAL MINISTRY RESOURCES VISIT

**www.jimwideman.com**

CPSIA information can be obtained at www.ICGtesting.com
Printed in the USA
LVOW11*2331180416

484194LV00002B/3/P